STEWART GILL

THE PAINTED SURFACE

A GUIDE TO PRODUCTS & TECHNIQUES FOR CONTEMPORARY MULTIMEDIA ARTISTS

REBECCA GILL

SG
PUBLISHERS

Contents

Author : Rebecca Gill

First Published 2005 by
Stewart Gill (Publishing) Ltd
Elgin Industrial Estate, Dunfermline, Fife
KY12 7SN Scotland, UK.
Telephone (UK +44) 0800 0277 921
www.stewartgill.com

Printed in the United Kingdom
ISBN : 1 - 905169- 00 - 0

section one
TECHNICAL
SPECIFICATIONS

Overview - how to identify the products

All art materials look, feel and behave differently. Understanding these differences ensures you get the most from your materials. Stewart Gill products can easily be identified by their attributes :

Appearance (what it looks like)
Application (how you use it)
Activation (what you do last to stabilise the product)

	Appearance	Application	Activation
Paints	Liquid state, viscous, coloured.	Use directly onto porous surface.	Dry naturally, heat-fix on fabrics.
Additives	Liquid state, white or colourless.	Use with a specific PAINT or EFFECT.	Dry naturally, then usually needs additional heat to activate.
Effects	Dry powders, flakes, gems, threads.	Use paint, glue, additives or stitch to adhere to surface.	Dry naturally, or use a heat-gun.
Tools	Plastic, metal, rubber, foam etc.	Specific usage instructions - see pack and adapt to suit.	Clean after use, retain packaging for instructions and storage.

The following pages

describe general attributes of Stewart Gill products, to help you identify, understand, and choose the most appropriate ones for your needs. After reading Section One, I definitely recommend making the Fabric Test Swatch first, even if you are very experienced with paints. Then try any of the Techniques or Gallery ideas that interest you - of course, you will discover additional and unique ways of working. Always keep notes in a visual journal as both successes and failures are equally valid for learning. And remember to break the rules occasionally, if not frequently!

Physical properties of the paints

Thick consistency for multiple techniques
For printing, stamping, stencilling, and fine line definition use the paint straight from the jar.
For silk & watercolour washes, resists and sponging, thin the consistency by diluting with water.

Multiple surfaces for multimedia artists
Providing each surface is porous, the same product & technique will give consistent results regardless of substrate. Intermixable colours layer effortlessly.

Water-based non-toxic formula
Dilute with water 3:1 for watercolour results and minimal colour reduction. Easy clean-up for tools, brushes and hands. EN71 compliance means the products are safe for use by children, and also on products intended for children, eg; clothes and toys.

Very soft surface handle
Painted fabric stays soft & supple, improving wash-permanence. Provides a perfectly smooth surface for machine-embroidery & embellishing.

Tough-Shine performance
Our glittery & metallic paints are pick-resistant and do not tarnish or melt with direct-to-surface heat.

True-Colour pigmentation
Using the best pigments ensures true jar-to-art colour & maximum UV ratings for vibrant, permanent results.

Anti-bleed formula
Colour stays put exactly where you want it, even on synthetics. You can even work wet-on-wet with minimal pigment migration. You don't need gutta or outliner pens, and have greater artistic control over the results.

Easy heat-fix with a dry iron
No fussy steaming or expensive equipment required. Quick and easy to heat-fix your fabrics, even across several painted layers.

Acid-free archival quality
Well regarded by industry professionals for exceptional colour & image durability. After initial heat-fixing, the painted surface is resilient and permanent. All paints can be hand or machine-washed, dry-cleaned, and tumble-dried. You can even iron direct-to-surface without fear of smudging or melting your artwork.

Surfaces & Techniques

WHAT SURFACES CAN I PAINT ?

Absolutely any porous surface is suitable, the only exceptions are metal & glass. We've successfully painted the following :

FABRICS
All unglazed fabrics - synthetic, natural and blends, available as yardage, threads, ribbons, and recycled trimmings. All plain and stretch weaves, stockings, hats, shoes.

CELLULOSE FIBRES
Untreated wood, bark, pasta shapes, dried beans, plant material (leaves, seedpods etc). Paper, card, vellum, paper pulp, paper clay, tapa cloth, hemp / fibre papers.

PROTEIN / ANIMAL PRODUCTS
Unpolished leather, suede, natural hide parchments, bone, shells, silk fusion.

AGGREGATES
Ceramics (unglazed), plaster, concrete, stones, sand, marble, chalk etc.

PLASTICS, POLYMERS
Firm plastics such as 'shrink' must be sanded prior to applying paint. All plastics & polymers must be heated after applying paint to ensure bonding.
Shrink plastic, plastic bags, cellophane, Tyvec, polymer clay and modelling compounds, polystyrene shapes and sheets, paper compounds (eg polystyrene clays).

FUSIBLES & FOAMS
"Bondaweb", inter-linings, "Vilene", buchram, synthetic quilting waddings & battings. Liquid latex & sheet rubber. Any CC foam (closed cell) such as "Memostafo", "Soft Sculpt", "Formy", "Magicstamp".

WHAT TECHNIQUES CAN I USE ?

We've had tons of fun experimenting with the following techniques, knowing there's lots more still waiting to be discovered :

HANDPAINTING & BLENDING
Traditional artists methods - watercolour, ink & wash, under-painting, over-painting.
Multiple layered coats of paint in translucent, glaze, & opaque finishes.
Impasto styles using thickeners and fillers.
Hand methods - sponge, rag, finger-paint, roller, spread & scrape with spatulas & tools.

PRINTING
Screen printing (all the paints use an average mesh size 43T, except Galactica glitter paint which requires size 11-15T)
Woodblock, linocut, monoprint, transfer techniques, used alone or in combination.
All printing techniques can be hand-coloured.

STAMPING
Commercially produced rubber art stamps & foam stamps.
Handmade carved erasers, linoblocks, vinyl, vegetable prints (fresh & dehydrated).
Handmade 'Closed-Cell' foam stamps (such as Memostafo or Magic Stamp) - heated and pressed into textures to imprint the pattern.
Handmade 3D stamps - using found objects assembled onto a block with adhesive.

STENCILLING
Commercially produced stencils are available in card, plastic, mylar and brass - each type is suitable for different products and techniques, so experiment to find your preference.
Alternatively you can design and cut your own from acetate or card.
Handmade stencils from found objects (doilies, sequin waste, crochet & lace, industrial waste eg; stripped circuit boards: anything flat with cutout areas).

BLENDING
Blend paint with other art mediums such as adhesives, gesso, varnishes, clays & fillers.

Colourise

MATTE, 30 SHADES, TRANSLUCENT & SEMI-OPAQUE

Colourise is especially versatile - WHY?

It contains lots of pigment to give rich strong colours - dilute with water 3:1 for easy blending and watercolour washes which maintain a strong colour yield.
Wet-on-wet direct painting holds sharp details and outline definition with minimal bleeding.

Shibori crinkled silk : *the high wash temperature is ideal for methods requiring steam or boiling water immersion.*

StyleStone & Rubber Stamping
Colourise is quick drying and perfect for all techniques which require quick-dry backgrounds for added surface embellishment. Fast workers can layer additional colours quickly without fear of smudging.

Available in (T) translucent or (S) semi-opaque coverage - see the shade chart. The shades are based on a traditional artists' palette, with both warm & cool versions of primary shades to ensure maximum mixing possibilities.

celcius
60

P

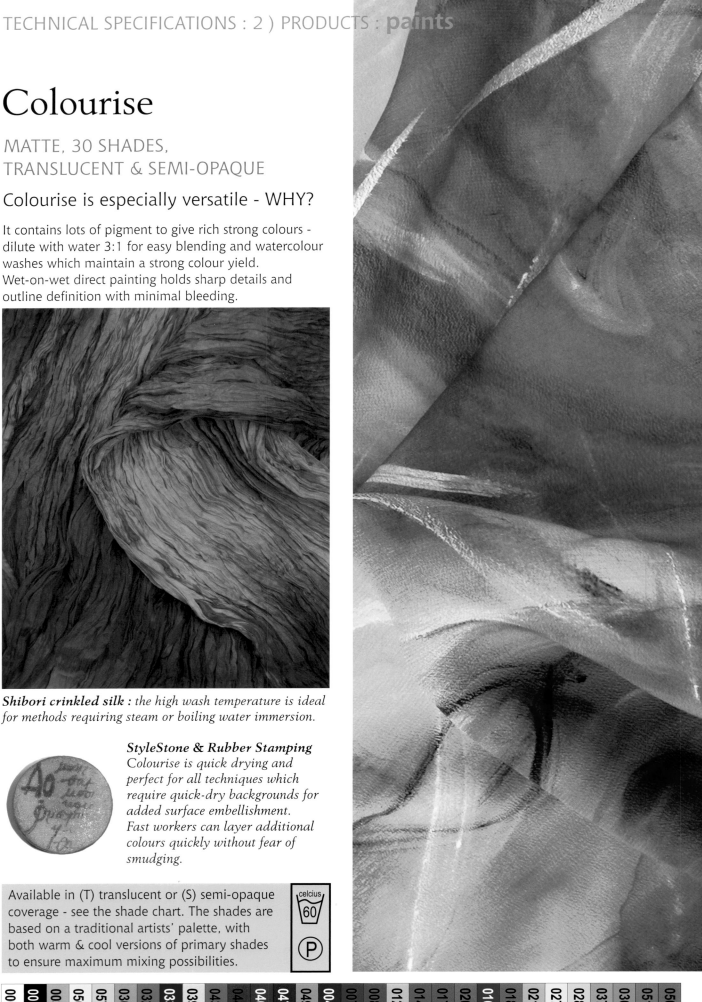

| 000 S | 001 S | 003 S | 056 S | 057 S | 030 T | 032 T | 033 T | 039 S | 043 T | 044 T | 046 T | 047 T | 049 S | 004 T | 007 T | 008 T | 012 S | 014 T | 017 T | 020 T | 016 T | 018 T | 021 T | 027 T | 028 T | 037 T | 036 T | 051 S | 050 T |

Colourise Additives

Performance boosters for especially demanding fabrics & advanced methods

EXTENDER MEDIUM

Increases the flow quota of Colourise while retaining the colour depth. Use as an alternative to diluting with water. It is suitable for hand painting techniques, where you want increased runnability without bleeding or feathering. Add sufficient to Colourise, mix well to desired consistency, and apply to your fabric.

ANTI-TRAVEL

This additive primarily works as a thickener to increase the viscosity of Colourise for screen and block printing.

Anti-Travel encourages Colourise to develop a good permanent bond on 'difficult' fabrics such as synthetics and wools. These fabrics are notorious for giving fabric paints a hard time, as the non-absorbent or fibrous surfaces prevent paint from adhering properly.

Anti-Travel also prevents any bleeding or feathering ("pigment migration") on very defined weave fabrics, such as twills and smooth satins. Make sure you follow the instructions on the label as it is super concentrated. Add just one drop of Anti-Travel per 5ml of Colourise and mix well to desired consistency.

technique
PRINT & PAINT

Edinburgh Castle Screenprint
Step 1 : Black C001 was mixed with Anti-Travel to thicken the paint ready for screenprinting. The hand-drawn castle image was developed into a photostencil screenprint on a size 43T mesh, and screened by hand. The printed image was left to dry, then heat-fixed.
Step 2 : Colourise was diluted in a palette, and painted in loose wash techniques to create this individual t-shirt design.

Colours used :
Olive C020
Ochre C030
Rust C032
Plum C044

Screenprinted Silk Scarf
Anti-Travel was added to Black C001 to control bleeding on the smooth surface of the silk crepe. Extender Medium was added to Cerise C043 to increase fluidity.

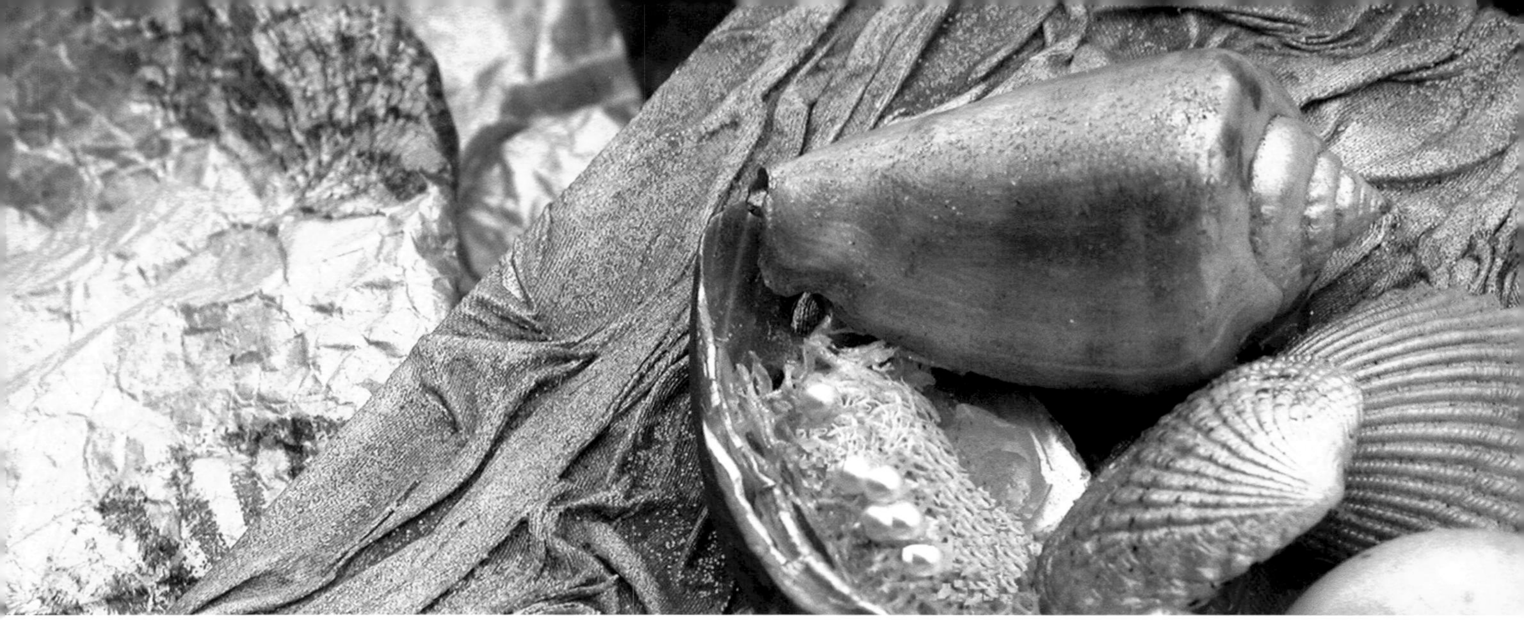

Pearlise

FROSTED, 10 SHADES, SEMI-OPAQUE

The subtle gleam and natural shades reflect the radiant glow of pearlescent seashells.

Pearlise can be thinned with water to create delicate shimmery glazes for highlights over a painted Colourise background. Alternatively, just paint directly onto a pre-coloured or printed matte background.
A heavy application creates a high degree of pearlescent shine and texture. Beautiful on three-dimensional surfaces where the glimmer is highlighted to full effect, such as interior fabrics, clothing, jewellery, boxes etc .

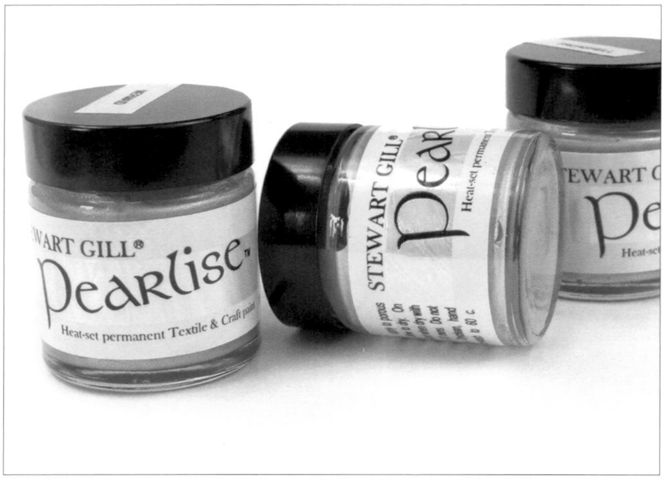

Image at top of page : Seashell Keepsake Box (detail)
Silk-wrapped box painted with Colourise C007, C014. White shoe-box tissue paper randomly sponged with Pearlise P07, P08, and stamped with a Memostafo shell stamp in Colourise C017. Shells & box texture highlighted with more Pearlise, and Galactica G323, G51.

P celcius 40

010 09 08 07 06 05 04 03 02 01

technique
PAPER BATIK

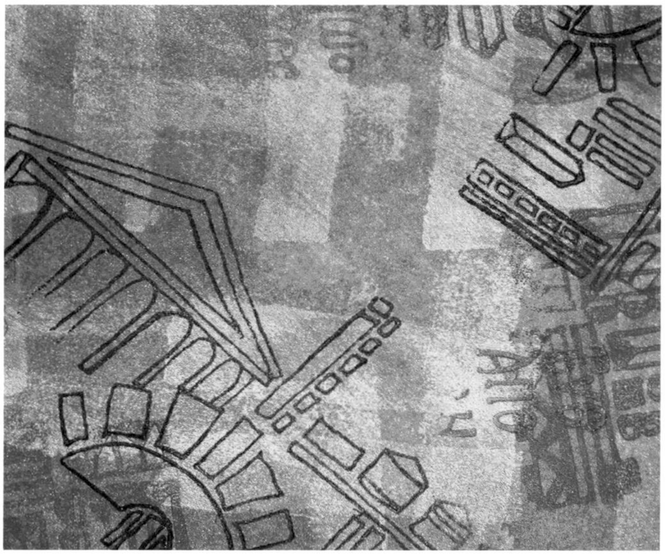

Step 1 : *Randomly apply White Pearlise P01 to white smooth card using foam stamps which have a bold surface pattern. (The Pearlise White needs to be quite visible, so don't choose stamps with intricate detail).*

Step 2 : *When thoroughly dry, gently sponge tiny amounts of 2-3 shades of Colourise over the surface.*
Blend the colours into each other for a marbled swirl.

NOTE : *If replicating this technique on fabric, make sure that you apply a fairly thick coating of Pearlise, as the fabric will be more absorbent than the card. Leave to dry naturally before heat-fixing. Then dilute the Colourise with water to sponge in effortlessly.*

VARIATIONS : *Experiment with any variation of stamp designs, paint and card colours.*

Alchemy

INTERFERENCE, 20 SHADES, SEMI-OPAQUE

Intensely magical and elusive, containing mica pearl particles, for an iridescent glint that resembles shimmering shot-silk.

A-01E *Opal*
Earth Palette - pink glow

A-16W *Seaspray*
Water Palette - green glow

A-06F *WhiteHot*
Fire Palette - gold glow

A-11A *WhiteMist*
Air Palette - blue glow

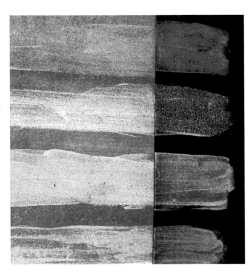

Once dry, Alchemy will reflect two different colour effects.
First you see the straight jar colour.
Secondly, as you move the painted object you will see an iridescent shimmer in either pink, green, gold or blue. This colour refraction effect is called 'interference.'
The interference colour glows stronger on a darker base.
Left : Interference effect
All the 'white' shades have been painted over both lilac card and black card to show how the colour intensifies.

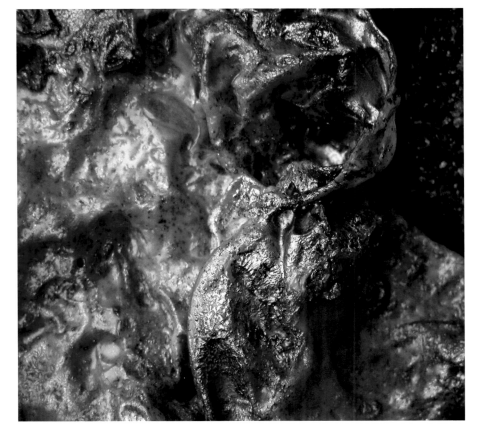

technique
MELT & MORPH

Laminating Plastic with Alchemy & Black Label Embossing Powders

Step 1 : *Use a spatula to apply Alchemy paints thickly onto flat sheets of hot-laminating plastic (the heat-sealing pouches designed for electric laminating machines).*

Step 2 : *Heat with a craft heat tool to melt & distort the plastic - the paint will bubble up and become more iridescent.*

Step 3 : *Sprinkle embossing powders over the surface and re-heat to melt.*

Colours used :
Alchemy (A15A Whirlwind, A14A Celestial, A04E Cobalt)
Black Label Embossing powder (AE14 Medallion, AE04 InterRed)

20W	19W	18W	17W	16W	15A	14A	13A	12A	11A	10F	09F	08F	07F	06F	05E	04E	03E	02E	01E

WATER - green refract	AIR - blue refract	FIRE - gold refract	EARTH - pink refract

Metamica

METALLIC, 20 SHADES, OPAQUE

Wonderfully resilient metallic paint that
stays shiny even through washing and heating.
Great news for multimedia textile embellishers -
your shiny bits will stay intact despite multiple paint & fabric layers.

Tyvec® Beads
*Painted strips of Tyvec® wrapped around a skewer, further paint layers applied,
then heated and spot-soldered for texture. Cooled, wrapped with wire & thread,
and finally more paint applied for extra shine.*

ARTIST : TRUDI TROUPE

It can be diluted with water, but this
reduces the shine as the metallic
particles are dispersed. So dilute
with care (to a maximum ratio of
water 2:1paint), unless you want a
very soft shimmery colour wash.
Extreme dilutions can however be
very effective on heavy watercolour
papers, and silk painting.

technique
BUBBLE & BLISTER

Step 1 : *Apply any shade very
thickly through a stencil (about 3mm
or 1/8") of paint build-up is needed.*

Step 2 : *While the paint is still wet,
blast it at close range with a heatgun.
This will cause a bubbling, blistering
raised texture. Smaller pattern areas
will hold their raised height better
than large surface areas, which tend
to flatten when cool.*

VARIATION SHOWN :
*Apply 2 shades wet-on-wet to achieve
mottled, marbled surfaces that
resemble distressed metal. Eg; M005
as a base, with M008 on top.*

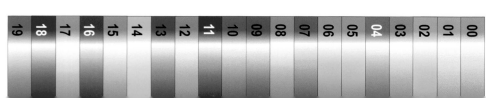

Galactica

GLITTER PAINT, 40 SHADES, OPAQUE

Ultrafine glitters impart a myriad of sparkles, for high performance and frequent laundering.

Galactica easily transforms your wearable art, street fashion, costumes and accessories. This unique paint contains no rubber, solvents or latex, so after the initial heat-fixing you can iron directly onto the painted image. It is extremely durable and scratch-resistant when heat-fixed.

The soft permanent surface allows additional embroidery and quilting, without fear of a tough surface or stray glitter damaging your sewing machine's bobbin housing.

Galactica shades are either pure glitter colours 'Classic' (WYSIWYG), or 'Interference' shades. All shades intermix with each other, for maximum sparkle when applied as the final layer. A softer sparkle is achieved if mixed with other paints. Do not water Galactica down, as this will dilute it's adhesive effect.

Note : The colour of wet Galactica looks nothing like the sparkle and brilliance the paint has when dry. Always choose your shades from the colour charts, and never from the jar contents.

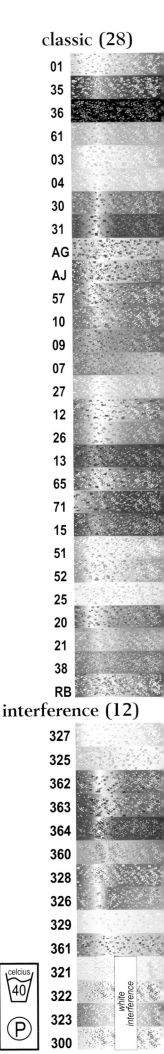

classic (28)

01
35
36
61
03
04
30
31
AG
AJ
57
10
09
07
27
12
26
13
65
71
15
51
52
25
20
21
38
RB

interference (12)

327
325
362
363
364
360
328
326
329
361
321
322
323
300

white interference

technique
SCRATCH & SCRAPE

Glittering Geometric Velvet

Step 1 : *Stick masking tape onto fabric to create positive and negative areas. Spread Galactica thinly over the unmasked areas with a spatula or palette knife.*

Step 2 : *Scratch patterns into the paint with a plastic fork. Remove tape carefully. Allow to dry and heat-fix. Remember to recycle the lovely glittery tape!*

celcius 40 / P

BYZANTIA

MULTIMEDIA PRODUCTS

A stunning collection of paints, effects, additives, diecuts and rubberstamps. Reflect the opulence & splendour of the Byzantine Empire - a time when making art was a sacred and revered ritual. Be inspired to create your own deeply personal iconic artworks.

Designing with the Byzantine Style in mind... Heavy goldwork inlaid with precious jewels, intricate filigree and mosaics, glorious enamelled treasures, religious and regal icons, illuminated manuscripts & inspirational frescoes.

Byzantia Cloisonné Paints

JEWELTONE METALLICS, 10 SHADES, OPAQUE

Extremely concentrated, shiny jewel tones that simulate Cloisonné Enamelling, in a water-based formulation. Very effective for highlights & intense areas of illumination.

Byzantia Collage : *Illuminata BP03, Seraphym BP09, Cardinale BP01, highlighted with brush, spatula and Artaglio Rubber Artstamps, over a background of Colourise, Fresco Flakes, and pencil.*

The Special Effect Products

BIJOUX BLENDS, GILDING CHIPS, FRESCO FLAKES, GLITTERATI, POLYGLITTER, GEMBELLISHMENTS, & BLACK LABEL EMBOSSING POWDERS.

Effects are the attention-grabbing decorative bits and pieces that will make your surfaces look stunning. They all require something LIQUID to adhere them to the surface, such as adhesives, paint, or molten embossing powder. Use alone, or combine for truly encrusted textures. Collage together, then over-paint, print or stamp. Trap between sheer layers such as fabric, vellum, acetate and handmade papers for mysterious, bejewelled encapsulations.

ARTIST : PADDY COSGRIFF

BIJOUX BLENDS

Simulated crushed gem colours blended from glass, quartz and marble, for very special projects. Use tools & protective gloves when handling the Bijoux, as the particles can be sharp, and not safe for children. Apply by sprinkling into Beadhesive glue, and press firmly into place with a spatula.
Bijoux blends give a wonderfully rich, crushed mosaic effect if added into the final layers of hot-melt embossing pieces. Press into polymer clays before baking and seal with varnish or embossing powder. Experiment as inlays with ceramics and Precious Metal Clay, or cast into resins and Friendly Plastic.

GILDING CHIPS

Bright and sparkly metallic PVC chunks create heavy-duty encrusted shine on cards, boxes, frames, die-cuts & jewellery mounts. Sprinkle into Beadhesive and allow to dry. Embed into embossing powders for rich glitzy layers. Trap between sheer fabrics, memory glass, and acetate sheets. Fuse between Glitterati for kaleidoscopic aperture mounts.

Note : Protect your iron with a heat resistant teflon / silicon sheet to avoid burning or damage.

FRESCO FLAKES

Matte flakes that resemble real bits of peeling paint, available in natural architectural shades. Fresco Flakes simulate authentic aging and weather-beaten textures.
Apply Colourise thickly with a spatula, then sprinkle Fresco Flakes over the wet paint to create mono-chromatic, minimalist textures.
Use un-inked rubber stamps to press into the wet background to render ancient graffiti-like impressions.
Mix with Beadhesive glue for super lumpy coagulated results that can be overpainted, stamped & stencilled. Crush for gritty tempera effects... you can even layer between sheer fabrics & stitch through them.

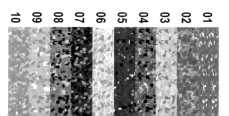

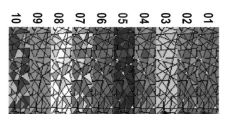

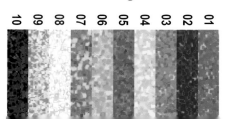

Glitterati Fusible Film & Fibres

IRIDESCENT ACID-FREE SPARKLES

Glitterati is a heat-responsive iridescent product, available in loose fibres, or sheets. The possibilities are endless, and endlessly sparkly!

technique
BASIC HEAT-FUSING METHOD

Step 1 : Take a very small amount of fusible Glitterati. Separate the strands and spread them out onto a piece of ordinary copier paper.
Note : The Holographic Metallic AJ & AG shades are NOT heat-fusible.

Step 2 : Place another paper sheet on top and iron for 2 seconds on a medium dry setting (NO STEAM). You can also use a teflon or silicon sheet to protect your iron.

Step 3 : Peel the top layer of paper back and Hey Presto! A beautiful delicate shimmery sheet of fused fibres that resembles a fine cobweb...

ARTIST : PADDY COSGRIFF

Above : Wrapped Fabric Bead
Painted fabric rolled and wrapped with Glitterati Fibres, coiled wire & beads.

Left : Faux Dichroic Opal
Glitterati Film sheets dipped in Ultragloss clear embossing powder with entrapped Bijoux Blends BB10 Opal.

HOLOGRAPHIC (not fusible) **HEAT-FUSIBLE FIBRES** **HEAT-FUSIBLE FILM**

AJ	AG		300	323	322	321	361	329	326	328	360	364	363	362	325	327		322	363	361

white Interference

white

ideas for use
COLD TECHNIQUES

Simple, effective ways to use Glitterati straight from the pack :

- add to paper-making vats
- layer into feltmaking & silk-fusion paper
- laminating onto ceramics, card & paper-maché
- hair & costumes for toys, puppets & art dolls
- knitting, crochet, weaving, embroidery
- cold-laminating with acetate sheets & clear stickers
- collage and scrapbooking
- tassels, beads & jewellery
- deep-embossing inclusions
- Christmas / special occasion decorations, ornaments & gift wrapping
- as a mount for card-toppers and 3D pieces such as polymer clay & shrink

ideas for use
HOT TECHNIQUES

After you've mastered basic heat-fusing, experiment further :

- Fuse several thinner bits together one at a time to build up a thicker, sturdier piece. Cut with decorative scissors, punch, stamp, stencil & paint to embellish further.
- Thicker fused pieces can also be stitched and shaped with heat into 3D objects such as lamps, hats, sculptures etc!
- Incorporate off-cuts and punched bits into Ultragloss molten embossing powder, or cold casting methods eg; resin.
- Dip scrunched & folded film sections into Ultragloss embossing powder to create faux dichroic 'opals'.
- Mix with 'filigree fluid' and iron heavily through a teflon sheet to make a frosted fabric that can be stitched, cut and punched through!

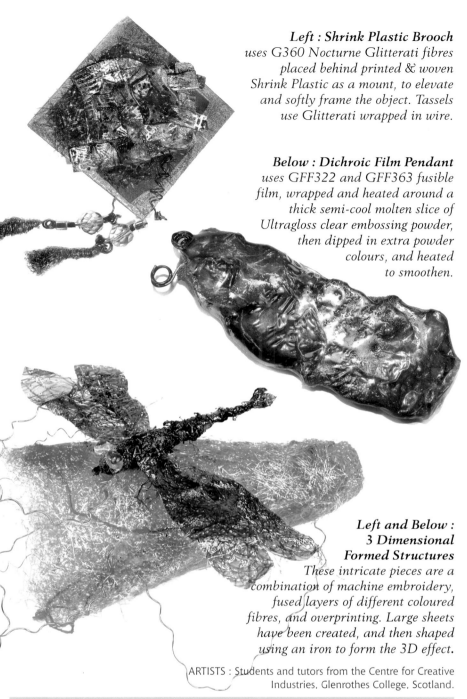

Left : Shrink Plastic Brooch
uses G360 Nocturne Glitterati fibres placed behind printed & woven Shrink Plastic as a mount, to elevate and softly frame the object. Tassels use Glitterati wrapped in wire.

Below : Dichroic Film Pendant
uses GFF322 and GFF363 fusible film, wrapped and heated around a thick semi-cool molten slice of Ultragloss clear embossing powder, then dipped in extra powder colours, and heated to smoothen.

Left and Below :
3 Dimensional
Formed Structures
These intricate pieces are a combination of machine embroidery, fused layers of different coloured fibres, and overprinting. Large sheets have been created, and then shaped using an iron to form the 3D effect.

ARTISTS : Students and tutors from the Centre for Creative Industries, Glenrothes College, Scotland.

Tip : you can recycle all the little off-cuts by simply fusing them into a fresh piece, or in between layers of Glitterati Film!

Black Label Embossing Powders

PREMIUM GRADE, 24 CLASSIC & SPECIALITY BLENDS

Embossing Powders are dry granules of heat-responsive resin which melt around 100-120° Celsius. With hundreds of different types available, Stewart Gill Black Label powders place an emphasis on superior grade quality, and original colour blends.

Embossing powders are not suitable for fabrics that require washing and ironing, as the heat of the iron will re-melt the powders. Sheer & synthetic fabrics, and speciality lightweight papers need extra care during the heating process, to avoid buckling & burning the surrounding area.

You will need a craft heat-gun to safely emboss with ease. Heat-guns are specifically manufactured to achieve the correct temperature of concentrated, directional heat, which ensures consistent, reliable results.

Note : Metamica, Pealise, Alchemy & Byzantia paints are all ideal to use as an embossing base, as the slower drying time of these paints gives you longer to apply the powders before the paint dries.

Safety Tips : *Always use tweezers to hold small items to protect your fingers from the heat-gun. Use spoons or sticks to decant powders, not your fingers. Prevent spillage by decanting a small amount of powder into the lid, instead of working from the open jar. Airborne particles present a potential risk of inhalation - therefore at all times be very careful when handling powders to prevent unwanted skin contact or respiratory inhalation. Adult supervision is recommended with children under 16 years of age.*

technique
BASIC EMBOSSING ON CARD

Step 1 : *Make a mark on smooth card with paint or embossing ink. Rubber stamps are ideal to begin with as you can clearly see the pattern that is embossed. Make sure the paint or ink is thinly applied and while it is still wet, liberally sprinkle with embossing powder to cover.*

Step 2 : *Shake excess powder onto a spare piece of paper. Use the spare paper to carefully return the powder to the jar to avoid wastage.*

Step 1 : *Activate the powder by heating with a craft heat-gun for approximately 20 seconds. Hold the gun at least 4 inches (10cm) away from the image to prevent burning. You will see the powder raise slightly, 'melt' into a smooth line and become shiny or change colour.*

INTERFERENCE (10)	METALLIC (6)	CLEAR (2)	BLENDS (3)	PATINAS (3)
01 02 03 04 05 06 07 321 322 323	08 09 10 12 13 14	21 11	15 16 17	01 02 03

white glitter blends

PolyGlitter

ACID-FREE, WASHABLE, 40 SHADES

Polyglitter comes in a gorgeous array of Classic and Interference colours, and can withstand high temperatures, making it ideal for both textiles and general crafts.

Available in all of the Galactica shades (see page 13) so you can perfectly match PolyGlitter and Galactica when working on cross-platform multimedia projects (eg; a glittered embossed jewellery with matching stencilled scarf). The Classic shades can withstand 100°C of non-contact heat, and the Interference shades up to 70°C. This heat-resistance makes PolyGlitter ideal for all textile applications that require laundering. It is a superb glitter for any craft application that needs close or prolonged heating, such as clay-baking, stamping, embossing, and obsessive burning & melting methods!

Use PolyGlitter sprinkled over glues, adhesive tapes, diecut sticky shapes and foam mounts for card crafts.

Use Filigree Fluid to either apply to rubber stamps, or create hand-drawn squeezy bottle patterns. Then coat with several shades of PolyGlitter and heat with a heat gun to raise up a sparkly pattern.

Add highlights to 3-D pieces by sprinkling into molten embossing powder, or clear varnish. And of course you can mix in with the paints for just a hint of shimmer.

Note : Avoid using sponges with PolyGlitter as the particles will clog the sponge.

technique
SPARKLING SCRAPBOOKS

Sparkly Scrapbook & Background papers
Step 1 : Apply Beadhesive lightly through a stencil onto a pre-patterned scrapbook page. Remove the stencil.
Step 2 : Sprinkle PolyGlitter over the Beadhesive. Shake off excess and dry naturally. Great for borders and trims, or use decorative punches to make quick & easy card toppers & tags. **NOTE :** *Middle section of photo shows an actual scrapbook page with a light application of Poly-Glitter. The end section shows a sample in progress, with a heavier application of PolyGlitter prior to thoroughly removing the excess. 'Less is definately More', in this case!*

Gembellishments

GEMS & ADORNMENTS

The perfect touch of luxury to adorn those extra-special projects - all are hand-picked for their beauty, and ability to withstand heat-gun techniques.

Freshwater pearls, Cubic-Zirconia, hand-made dichroic glass cabochons, semi-precious gemstones, Venetian mille fiori, marcasites...
Mount onto greeting cards, pictures, and book covers with Beadhesive. Arrange fantastic motifs on textiles for costumery, or jewellery. Embed directly into clays, resins, friendly plastic & embossing powder. Set in traditional jewellery mounts, or even onto ceramics, glass, or metal.

Purple Pearls (detail) : Byzantia paints (BP06, BP09) & Embossing powder AE08, with Sapphire Bijoux BB05 & pearls applied to Beadhesive.

Beadhesive

SUPER STRONG JEWEL ADHESIVE

Extremely effective adhesive for all the EFFECTS, but especially good at holding beads & gems onto textiles.

Squeeze directly onto the fabric from the nozzle applicator, sprinkle on beads, sequins, glitter or any of the Effects range. Press down securely and leave to dry naturally. Iron on medium-hot for 5-10 minutes on reverse side once dry.
Alternatively, for heavily-encrusted effects, use a generous application and place in preheated oven as soon as applied. Bake immediately at 150°C for 5 minutes only. Take care not to burn the cloth. Remember to use only genuine gemstones, glass and textile-glitter, as plastic beads and glitters will burn!

Filigree Fluid

PATINA EFFECT SUBTLE EXPANDING MEDIUM

Used alone or with embossing powders, this gives a raised textural effect when heated with a heat-gun.

It can be coloured with all Stewart Gill paints, by buffing the raised edges. Formulated to be slower-drying, and more stable on textiles, than other puff mediums. You can squeeze the fluid straight from the bottle for freeform textural patterns, or apply thickly to stamps via a latex sponge or Stylus Pen.

technique
FAUX CLOISONNÉ

Step 1 : *Hold the bottle upside down, with the applicator nozzle nearly vertical. Squeeze the bottle very slightly as you 'draw' to release the fluid in thin lines. Geometric and abstract patterns are very easy and effective - try not to 'overdraw' by filling up the whole space - keep empty areas between the fluid lines.*

Step 2 : *Apply metallic or patina embossing powders over the fluid while still wet, then heat to "Rise & Shine". This creates a wonderful raised semi-shiny effect that can simulate ancient filigree jewellery.*

Step 3 : *Once cool, use a fine brush to paint the Cloisonné Jewel Tone paints in between the raised areas. Use a thick application of paint - the raised Filigree Fluid will act like walls to contain the deep paint level.*

Craft Tools

TOP QUALITY, FUNCTIONAL STYLING

Little Helper Jewel Tool
5-prong pick-up tool holds tiny beads & Gembellishments easily for threading and embedding.

LH05

Long Reach Tweezers - these tweezers grip on when you let go, leaving your hands free for ease and safety during hot work.

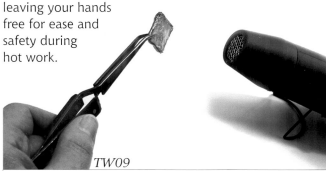

TW09

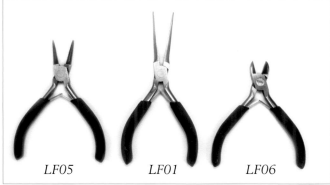

LF05 *LF01* *LF06*

Jewellery & craft pliers - Insulated-handle for safety and comfort. Various styles for cutting, shaping & coiling with art & jewellery wire.

Spatula Sets - 5 piece plastic art spatulas for spreading & scraping, tweaking and turning work.

Art Palettes - 2 sizes with areas for colour mixing.

Diecut Shapes

ACID-FREE BYZANTIA STYLED SHEETS

Available in Black or White, warp-resistant board. Use with any product from the Paint & Effect ranges for : Jewellery, Collage, Scrapbooks, MiniFrames, Books, Cardmaking, Boxes, Costumery etc...

ARTIST : DOROTHY ADAMS

Iconic Assemblage
Byzantia paint BP09 Seraphym BP06 Constantine, Gilding Chips GC10 Phoenecia, Embossing Powder M008 Gold

TINY TREASURES
ACID-FREE MINI GIFTBOX BLANKS

Available in Matte Black or White, 320gsm smooth card stock, perfect for colouring, stamping & embellishing.

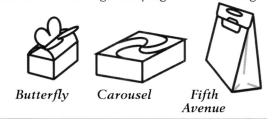

Butterfly   *Carousel*   *Fifth Avenue*

Deep-Etch Rubber Artstamps

FINER DETAIL DESIGNS FOR TRADITIONAL DEEP-ETCH RUBBER STAMPING

Our unmounted rubber stamps are available either as singles, or in themed sets. Each set contains several images co-ordinated to create great looking projects.

Unmounted sizes available :
A4 (210 x 295mm / 8 ¼ x 11 ¼ inches).
A5 (146 x 210 mm / 5 ¾ x 8 ¼ inches).
A6 (74 x 105mm / 4 ¼ x 5 ¾ inches).
CD (117 x 140mm / 4 ½ x 5 ½ inches).

Mounting Methods

FLEXIBLE OPTIONS

If you prefer your stamps mounted, there are now many ways to achieve it. It depends on whether you need your mounted stamps to be flexible, or rigid.

MEMOSTAFO
Melt & Mount Stamping Foam
Attach the foam sheet to the reverse side of the rubber sheet with spray adhesive, or double-sided adhesive tape. Then simply cut through both layers when you trim your stamps. Memostafo allows extra cushioning and grip, without losing the flexibility for bending around shapes, or the ability to apply selective pressure to random areas.

MAGNESIVE
Magnetic Self-Adhesive Sheets
These are extra strong magnetic sheets, capable of holding large stamps (eg; the Artaglio which are much heavier than standard stamps). Magnesive are ideal for temporary mounts for use with a magnetic block system. The stamps easily pop on and off the block for quick stamping, cleaning and storage. Simply peel off the adhesive backing paper and stick Magnesive sheets to the back of the rubber sheet. Trim through both sheets at the same time with scissors. And of course, it's perfect for backings on pins and fridge magnets!

Right : If you prefer traditional wooden blocks, simply glue or tape the rubber stamp on. You can use Memostafo as the middle layer of cushioning foam. Alternatively, acrylic blocks and static-cling mounting foam are a great system if you want viewing clarity combined with easy re-positioning.

*Selection shows (clockwise) : PB13, KS1, MS4 Winter, MS1 Spring, KS3, and KS2. **Below** : wood-mounted RG3*

Artaglio Rubber Artstamps

SUPER DEEP-ETCH, UNMOUNTED, ECLECTIC DESIGNS

These are the deepest stamps ever! Doubling the standard profile depth, Artaglio make brilliant impressions for multimedia stamp art.

Why Deep? To give the cleanest, sharpest print on textiles, heavy or textured surfaces, and hot-melt enamelling & moulded clay impressions.

Why Unmounted? Artaglio can bend around curved surfaces, offer variable pressure for stamping into uneven surfaces and clays, and for partial area stamping for random pattern techniques. Easy to clean by soaking in hot, soapy water.

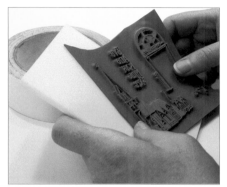

Artaglio are designed to be used unmounted, but you can quickly attach the sheets to 'Memostafo' foam with double-sided tape, for a flexible temporary mount.

With sharp scissors, carefully trim as close as possible to the design, leaving about 2mm clearance. The unmounted stamp is now ready to ink-up.

The inking-up method is the same no matter whether your stamp is mounted or unmounted.

It's easiest to use a latex foam sponge to apply the paint to the stamp, and not a paintbrush. This prevents excess paint clogging in the recesses of the rubber. Clearsnap ® Colorbox Stylus Pens with applicator foam tips are perfect for inking up stamps cleanly and evenly.

Use the paint lid like a mini palette to dip the pen into. Always apply paint to stamps with an up and down dabbing motion, similar to a traditional inkpad, to achieve the cleanest, sharpest stamped image.

Left : Layered Artaglio Picture
Byzantia paint (BP09, BP06) brushed randomly on background. Artaglio stamps embossed with M008 powder. Paper clay emblem impressed with stamp, painted with diluted shades. Additional block-embossing scratched to reveal base colour.

Modular System Stencils

6" SQUARE REPEAT-DESIGN STENCILS FOR SCRAPBOOK & QUILTING LAYOUTS

Achieve perfectly aligned all-over patterns on almost any surface, easily. You have total creative freedom to use the stencils as single stand-alone motifs, borders, continuous lengths, or texture masks.

MS is made from laser-cut Mylar to give :

- intricate high-detail images
- a thin paint build for professional results
- strong, long-lasting material quality
- repeated uses without loss of detail
- easy to bend around curved surfaces eg; lamps, vases
- easy clean-up with warm water and mild detergent

ARTISTS : FIONA KELLY & RG

All MS stencils have easy Registration Marks

(L)	Corners
(X)	Centre axis or centre point
(■)	Alignment points
(T)	¼ inch (6mm) seam allowance

For Scrapbooking

Create unique personalised background papers
Use a single stencil placement for a 6" page, or align the stencil 4 times to create a 12" layout.

For Quilting

Position the stencils centrally for stand-alone motifs on a single block.
Align the stencils using the registration marks to create all-over patterned yardage for cutting and piecing.
The outer dimensions of the stencils are 6 ½" including seam allowances. If you cut your fabric exactly to the outer edge of the stencil, and sew ¼" in from the cut edge, the finished internal area is exactly 6". All the registration points fall within the seam allowance, so will not be visible in the finished piece.

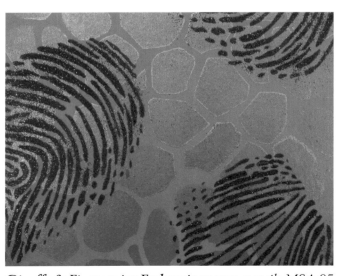

Giraffe & Fingerprint Embossing : uses stencils MSA-05 and MSA-09 from the Original Skins collection, with Colourise Vermillion C036, Metamica Brass M002, and Marcasite AE16 embossing powder.

For General Crafts

Suitable for use on polymer clays, card, paper, textiles, home décor, glass, ceramic, walls and more!

How to use the Registration Marks

Firstly, decide what type of pattern you are going to build : single stand-alone motifs, repeating borders, or all-over continuous patterns. The type of pattern chosen will depend on the intended use in your particular project.

Single Motifs in Random Placement
Position the stencil anywhere you like - but take care on garments to avoid drawing unwanted attention to body-specific areas. Bulky seams can cause the stencil to smudge, so it may be best to unpick the seam. Open it out flat, then stencil, heat-fix, and re-sew the seam to join.

Rotating / Repeating Motifs for Borders
Choose a single registration point - usually either the centre-axis, or one of the baseline corners, to act as the pivotal point upon which you locate the movement of the stencil. You can then repeat / rotate your stencil around this point, or along a continuous baseline (if a border). If your stencil overlaps onto an area of fresh paint, the second print may cause smudging. To avoid this, stencil every alternate repeat - mark all the registration points before you start. First, stencil Repeats 1,3,5,7 etc. When dry, go back and stencil Repeats 2,4,6...etc.

All-Over Continuous Patterns
It is very important that you trial your registration marks, as some of the designs (eg; Ikebana) have a variety of repeat pattern combinations possible from the one stencil.

1   Use special fabric fade-away pens or tailors chalk if working on fabric; light pencil on paper.
2   Mark the corner points first on your design area.
3   Mark the alignment points on your design area.
4   Apply paint to stencil, carefully remove stencil.
5   Place stencil back down on the work, aligning the registration points to the pencil marks from the previous stencil.

The second print from the same stencil should locate with the first as follows :
The corner points of the side you have just stencilled, should match to the alignment points of the opposite side (eg; side A1=A2). Stencil in straight rows only, from either top to bottom or side to side. When one whole length or width of your design area has been covered by a single row, repeat the process on the second row along. Work in the same direction as the previous row, making sure the B-sides registrate in the same way.
The row direction doesn't matter, as long as it is consistent .

1- Pencil in registration points

2- Apply paint to 1st Repeat

3- Apply paint to 2nd Repeat

4- Peel stencil away from painted area

Applying Stewart Gill paints through stencils

These instructions are for Colourise, Metamica, Pearlise, Alchemy & Byzantia paints, but will equally apply to any other viscous water based paint.

1- Spray adhesive on reverse

3- Using the lid as a mini palette

5 & 6- Applying & blending paint

7- Remove stencil away from paint

1. Apply repositionable spray adhesive lightly to reverse of stencil. Allow adhesive to dry for one minute before using the stencil. If you have used too much adhesive, blot the excess onto a separate piece of clean dry fabric.

2. With adhesive-side down, press firmly to ensure the stencil is securely in place.

3. Using a dense latex sponge, lightly dab into the jar lid to pick up a small amount of paint. The Colorbox® Stylus tool with inter-changeable white foam tips is the perfect accessory for stencilling. Dab the tip straight into the jar lid - use it like a mini-palette.

4. Dab the sponge onto a palette (or large uncut area of the stencil) to blot excess paint and distribute evenly). Use the palette to blend colours for multi-coloured or graduated effects.

5. Dab the paint over the stencil, using a gentle up and down motion. Take care not to stencil over the edges (use masking tape as a barrier).

6. Use a clean sponge to blend additional shades. Apply colours from light to dark to maintain colour purity. If the first colour has partially dried you can layer additional shades as glazes (eg metallic or pearlescent highlights)

7. Gently peel off stencil when finished. Clean carefully with warm water and detergent. Stubborn adhesive on the reverse can be removed with white spirit.

Store flat in a plastic bag or sealed box.

Applying Galactica paint through stencils

Intricate results can be achieved effortlessly to create unique luxurious surfaces.

If stencilling on thick-pile fabrics like velvet, wool, fleece, velour, etc; allow the spray adhesive to dry for several minutes before positioning the stencil. Overly tacky adhesive will leave traces on the fabric and could remove the surface pile.

Tip : Try mixing several shades together on the same stencil - this produces a lovely shimmery 3D effect.

Spatula held at a low angle, swiped across the stencil

Scraping excess paint off with spatula at vertical angle

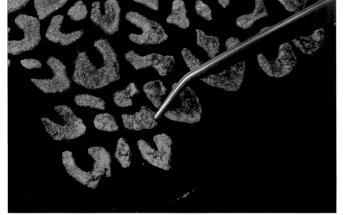

Lift off minor smudges at once with a sharp tool

Step 1 : *Using a kitchen spatula, take a small amount of Galactica and spread gently and evenly over the design area. Hold the spatula at a low angle (about 30 degrees).*

Step 2 : *Similar to icing a cake - aim to cover the design with as few strokes as possible to ensure smooth, thin coverage with no bleed-through.*

Step 3 : *Remove the excess paint and return to the jar. A thinner paint coverage gives a flatter, more professional result.*

Step 4 : *Remove the stencil. If used on fabric, allow at least 2 hours drying before heat-fixing. 24 hours is recommended on thicker / pile fabrics. No fixing is needed on craft items / suede paper etc.*

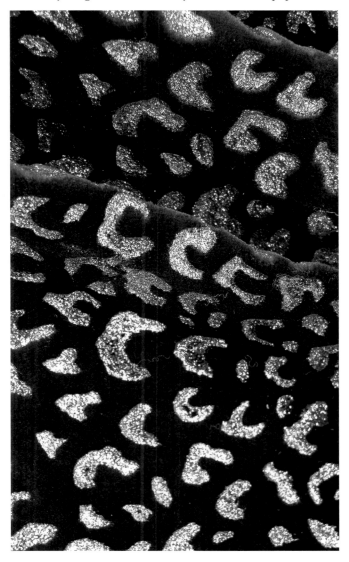

Specific Fabric Issues

PREPARING YOUR FABRIC FOR PAINT

It is very important to pre-scour your fabrics to thoroughly remove all surface conditioners before applying any paint or dye products. Failure to do this may result in the paint not achieving a good chemical bond when heat-fixed, and subsequently washing off.

Most fabrics contain 'sizing' or starches, to give the cloth a crisp drape and enable them to look better when you buy them. Other fabrics such as wools and silks may have retained natural oils, fats, or seracin in the fibres despite the production processes.

All Stewart Gill paints are designed to work on every 'untreated' fabric, both naturals, synthetics, and material blends. 'Untreated' means having no surface-conditioning treatments residual in the fibres. You need to 'pre-scour' (ie; remove the surface conditioners) before you apply any paints or dyes.
The best way to pre-scour fabrics is to gently wash in a lukewarm solution of a PH-neutral detergent such as Synthrapol or Metapex. These remove the starches and oils gently, without adding any other chemicals normally found in household washing detergents.

Choose 100% cotton for all initial tests with unfamiliar paints. It's easier to test the performance of different paints on fabric that is really brilliant white, very smooth-surfaced, with a tight, close weave.

Comparing different brands by testing the same methods on the same fabric type is a reliable indicator of each product's capabilities. When you are satisfied

that you understand the basic qualities of a paint on 100% cotton, then test the same methods on to a variety of other fabric blends.

Except on pure wool and some synthetic blends, all Stewart Gill paints will achieve the same results regardless of surface, so you can do great life-like visual mock-ups or trials in your workbooks, and your final projects on fabric will be true to your original vision.

PREPARING YOUR WORK SURFACE

Working onto a slightly padded surface is my essential recommendation to anyone involved in textile decoration.

Use flat rubber carpet underlay, or a length of foam-backed vinyl fabric, and lay directly onto the worktable. If your work space is limited, consider a cut up section of 'Closed-Cell' foam to fit. (Ultra-thin camping mattresses are ideal).

Next lay a thick sheet of smooth polythene, and finally a pre-washed and ironed sheet of thick, smooth,

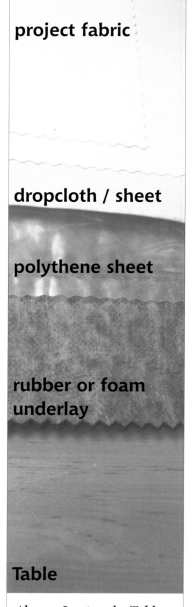

project fabric

dropcloth / sheet

polythene sheet

rubber or foam underlay

Table

Above : Laying the Table
Shows the correct order for layering the various items needed to prepare your work surface.

closely-woven 100% cotton. The surface must be absolutely smooth without wrinkles. This top layer, the 'dropcloth,' can be washed between painting sessions, or used underneath sheer fabrics to create a duplicate copy of each painted length (ie; If you were creating an outfit requiring different weights of fabric painted to the same effect).

Choosing brushes & tools

You will need a variety of good quality brushes - this does not necessarily mean expensive - but choosing the right brushes for the job.

Stewart Gill paints are thick, and need a firm yet supple brush to support the paint and aid flow when creating washes. Watercolour & Silk painting brushes are far too floppy for Stewart Gill paints, and oil brushes tend to be too stiff to allow good paint flow. For most fabrics I recommend white nylon or golden taklon bristles - very reasonably priced, but supple for beautiful blends, and strong enough to last through some pretty intense brushwork. The white nylon bristles are specifically designed for fabric painting. The bristles are slightly stiffer and stronger than the taklon, and are longer wearing on fabrics which tend to 'rough-up' other softer bristles. Choose a variety of sizes and head styles, such as flat, round, & filbert shapes. Experiment to find the best ones for your particular style.

Before each painting session, and always with new brushes, soften the bristles by steeping in warm water for 5 minutes prior to use - this swells the fibres, making them more absorbent and ready to load up with paint. After steeping, blot the excess water out, or your paint will become diluted.

In the **Last Words** section, I have included a list of essential items I simply cannot do without. Brush sizes are included in this list to help you with your selections.

No modern crafter can really be without the contents of the kitchen drawer - from recycled polystyrene trays, margarine lids and bits of sponge, rags and scouring pads to knives & forks, old whisks, string and spatulas - these items form the mainstay of our toolkits. Always scavenge at home first before venturing forth to the shops - who knows what treasures lie waiting for you!

The Fabric Test Swatch

YOU WILL NEED:

Fabric 12" (30cm) square of pre-scoured white cotton
Tools flathead / pointed brushes, spatula
Sponges assorted types, eg sea-sponge, foam, latex etc
Stamps one rubber, one foam
Paint 2 jars Colourise (any shade)
1 jar (any shade) of each of the following : Metamica, Pearlise, Galactica, & Byzantia paint
1 jar each of the Alchemy whites: (A01E, A06F, A11A, A16W)
Water (warm) in large jar
Rags / paper towels
Domestic iron

RELIABLE & REPEATABLE TESTING

Valid swatch tests are those that can accurately and reliably be repeated. Documenting your process for each fabric surface, method & product is essential for developing a thorough & professional knowledge base.

Once you have tested the paints on 100% cotton, it is useful to carry out the same test on 100% wool, 100% silk and 100% polyester. Then adapt the test for any specific techniques, fabric blends, or other surfaces you plan to use. Making duplicate swatches (ie; two of everything) allows you to keep a pre-washed comparison when testing wash-fast performance.
NOTE : Artists working in non-textile mediums should adapt this test to suit the specific surface being used.

BEFORE YOU BEGIN :

Prepare the fabric and work surface as described on page 28. Stretch the fabric out and smooth down onto work surface to ensure no wrinkles appear. Soften your brushes by steeping in medium-hot water for 5 minutes, then drain and blot. You are now ready to begin!

Making the Test Swatch

Test 1 : Bleed Levels
Use the flat head taklon brush and apply a straight stroke of Colourise taken neat from the jar. Do not water it down - the aim is to make a defined line edge.
Test Criteria : this tests the paints potential for 'capillary attraction', or bleeding into the surrounding fibres.

Test 2 : Pigment Concentration
Dilute the Colourise in a palette to a 90% concentration with a little bit of water. This means 9 parts paint to 1 part of water. Paint a straight stroke in this concentration. Add more water to dilute and continue painting a stroke of each dilution until the paint is very pale, or only a 10% concentration.
Test Criteria : This will test the pigment concentration of the particular shade, and the increased bleed levels when diluted.

Test 3 : Absorption Rate
Paint a large area of Colourise diluted to 30% concentration. While still damp, choose another contrasting shade of Colourise. Using neat, paint a sharp line of the contrast shade right through the damp paint, and out onto the dry fabric. Paint a variety of thin and thick patterns & dots. Assess for bleeding or feathering of the paint into the surrounding fabric.
Test Criteria : This tests the specific capillary attraction of the fibres for the specific wetness of the paint (ie; how quickly the diluted paint will dry on the fabric). This informs whether a wet-on-wet painting technique will be suitable.

Test 4 : Colour Blending
Paint solid, undiluted areas of Colourise several inches apart. Dilute each colour in a palette, and paint into the gap, layering more alternately to achieve a graduated colour blend.
Test Criteria : This tests the blending ability of the paint, relative to the specific fibres, and suitability for handpainting.

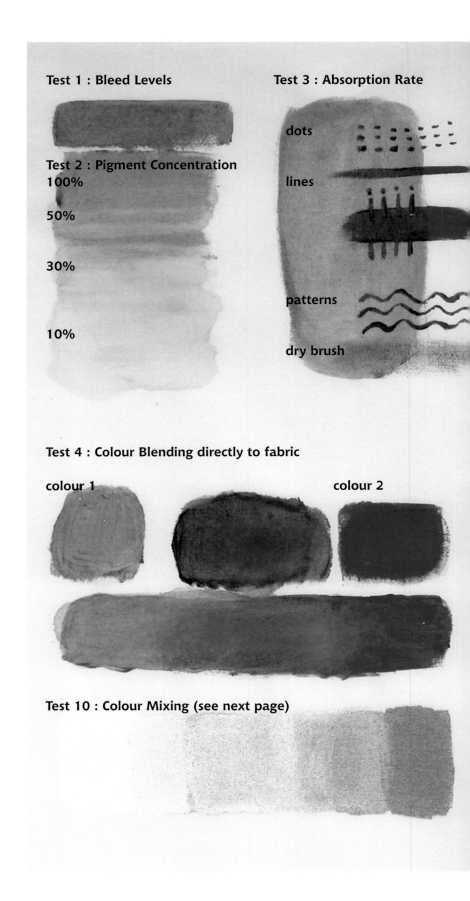

Test 1 : Bleed Levels

Test 3 : Absorption Rate

Test 2 : Pigment Concentration
100%

50%

30%

10%

dots

lines

patterns

dry brush

Test 4 : Colour Blending directly to fabric

colour 1

colour 2

Test 10 : Colour Mixing (see next page)

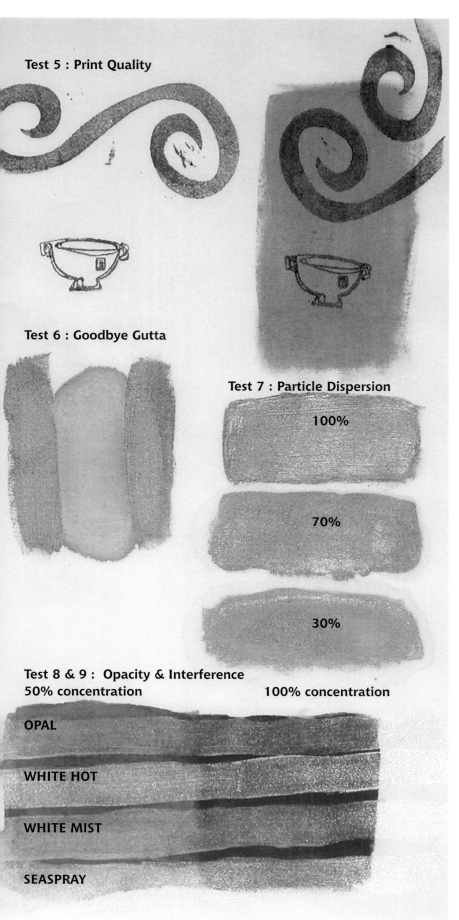

Test 5 : Print Quality

Test 6 : Goodbye Gutta

Test 7 : Particle Dispersion

100%

70%

30%

Test 8 & 9 : Opacity & Interference
50% concentration   100% concentration

OPAL

WHITE HOT

WHITE MIST

SEASPRAY

LEAVE ENTIRE SWATCH TO DRY FOR 24 HOURS, THEN HEAT-FIX, & WRITE REFERENCE NOTES DIRECTLY ONTO THE FABRIC FOR FUTURE REFERENCE.

Test 5 : Print Quality
Stamp one impression each with the rubber and foam stamps using neat Colourise. (Inking-up instructions p.23)
Test Criteria : This tests both the specific paint & fabric's ability to hold a detailed image. **Note :** *Smoother surfaces such as cotton sateen, silk & polyester satin, and card always give a sharper impression.* Repeat Step 5 using the Metamica, Alchemy, Pearlise & Byzantia paints.

Test 6 : Goodbye Gutta
Paint two lines of neat Metamica, with a defined inside edge. Leave to dry for 20 minutes. Then 'flood-fill' the inside area with a 30% concentration Colourise.
Test Criteria : This tests bleed-control & the paints ability to act as it's own gutta.

Test 7 : Particle Dispersion
Paint a solid stripe of 100% Metamica. Next paint a 70% concentration, and then a 30% concentration.
Test Criteria : This tests the dispersion of metallic particles and the correlation between dilution and shine reduction. Repeat Step 7 with Pearlise, Byzantia, and one of the white Alchemy shades.

Test 8 & 9 : Opacity & Interference
Paint a large square of colourise where one half is a 50% concentration, and the other half a 100% concentration. Allow to dry. With a clean brush, paint on each of the white alchemy shades, starting on the bare fabric, and continuing onto both the coloured sections.
Test Criteria : This tests the opacity levels of the paint, and the interference qualities relative to the background shade depth.

Test 10 Colour mixing :
Paint a square of neat Pearlise White onto your fabric. In a palette add a tiny hint of Colourise to the Pearlise. Paint this tinted colour onto your fabric. Add more Colourise gradually, painting the tints onto the fabric, until the tints reach maximum pigment saturation (ie until the Pearlise cannot get any deeper).
Test Criteria : This test measures the correlation between pigment quantity and shimmer-reduction, and informs you when mixing your own shades. It also tests the compatibility between different paints.

Variation : Experiment with mixing and layering Galactica with the other paints, to see the effects when particles are mixed.

Heat-fixing and Laundering

Heat-fixing your painted fabrics will ensure your creative efforts will last for generations, throughout repeated wearing, wash & dry cycles.

All fabric surfaces must be heat-fixed to set the paints if washing / dry-cleaning is necessary. On non-washable surfaces simply air-dry, or use a heat-gun to speed-dry. Each paint has washing & dry-cleaning symbols on the relevant page in the Products section of this book, and also on the colour charts available in stores. Temperatures given are in °Celsius, and are suitable for automatic washing machines. We recommend non-biological mild detergents without abrasives, salts or bleaching agents.

If hand washing, gently soak, and rinse. Take special care, particularly with metallic and glittery particle paints, not to rub or scrub during washing, as this can abrade the painted surface causing it to come off.
All textile pieces should be tested prior to committing to the final project - prepare a working sample that is as close a possible in application, colours, and fabric to the finished piece. Launder in the same way as you would with the finished item to check for suitability.

technique
IRON-FIXING INSTRUCTIONS   FOR COLOURISE, PEARLISE, METAMICA, ALCHEMY & BYZANTIA

Step 1 : *Make sure fabric is completely dry, place face-down on ironing board. Protect your board with a cloth.*
Step 2 : *Set the iron to the correct maximum dry temperature for the particular fabric type. For example, cottons, viscose, linen, etc can withstand very hot settings, whereas polyester, silk, wool and wool mixes, and nylons etc all require cool-medium settings.*
NOTE : *Always use a dry iron, never steam, for the initial fixing. You must avoid creating moisture through excessive heating. Moisture generated will encourage uncooked paint to become semi-liquid again. To prevent moisture building up, you can 'air' the piece every 30 seconds or so - lift the cloth briefly away from the board to circulate fresh air.*
Step 3 : *Iron on the reverse side of the fabric for 2-3 minutes. Always iron on the back first when doing the initial heat-fixing. The heat draws the paint into the fibres and makes the bond more permanent. Each section will take 2-3 minutes, so larger pieces will take longer overall.*
Step 4 : *Then iron on the front for a further 2-3 minutes. You can use a cloth to protect your iron if you wish. After the initial heat-fixing and the first washing, the painted surface can be ironed directly, without the need for a cloth.*

ALTERNATIVE METHODS FOR LARGE PIECES :

Ironing press - this speeds things up greatly, but remember not to use any steam. You can iron for 2-3 minutes to 'sear' and then put it in a
Commercial tumble dryer - these are much hotter than domestic dryers; tumble for 30 minutes to 1 hour.
Oven baking - at 130 degrees Celsius for 20 minutes. The cloth must be well-wrapped in protective Teflon or newsprint / clean cotton sheeting so that nothing touches the oven sides. **WARNING:** needs constant watching and turning to avoid burning (unfortunately learnt from bitter personal experience!)

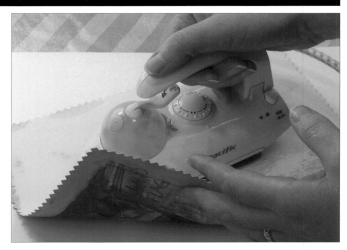

additional notes
IRON-FIXING GALACTICA

Galactica must be left for at least 2 hours, preferably overnight to ensure the paint is thoroughly dry. Allow 24 hours for velvets & deep pile fabrics. Fixing instructions for Galactica are the same as for the other paints, be sure to never use steam. The white Interference shades must be fixed at a lower temperature to avoid burning.

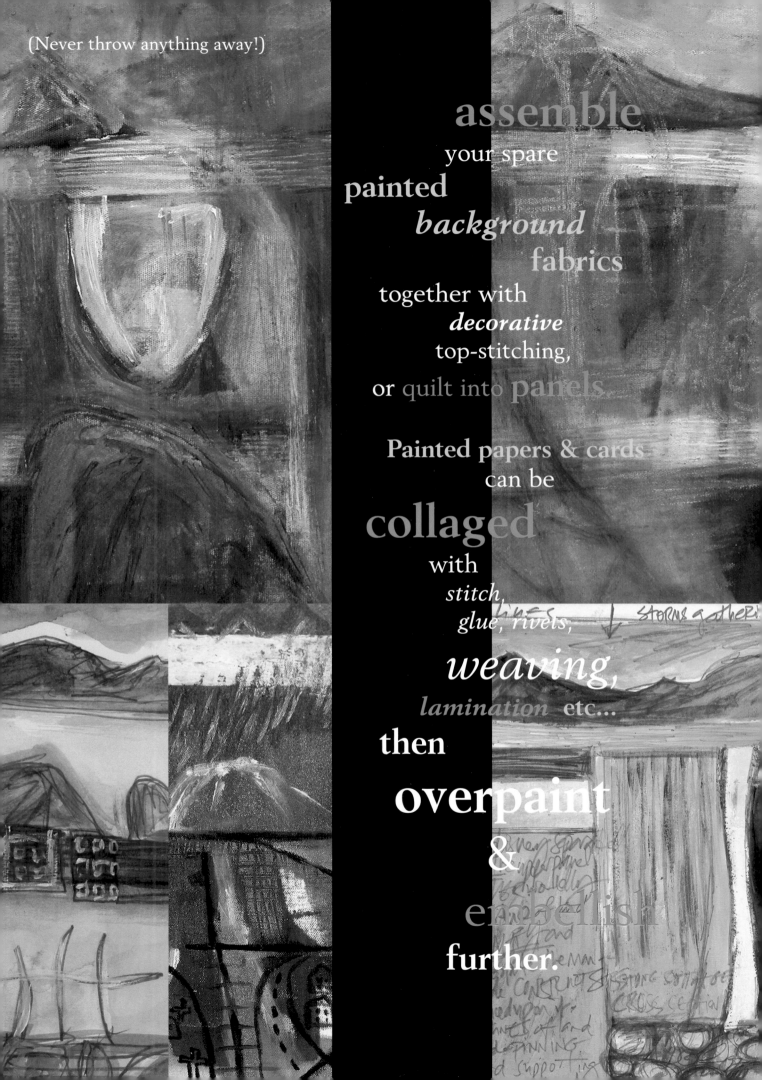

(Never throw anything away!)

assemble
your spare
painted
background
fabrics
together with
decorative
top-stitching,
or quilt into panels

Painted papers & cards
can be

collaged

with
stitch,
glue, rivets,
weaving,
lamination etc...
then

overpaint
&
embellish
further.

All about Colour

Understanding the basic theory will take the confusion out of colour to help you successfully mix your own paint shades.

PAINT-COLOUR THEORY
The visual appearance of any paint depends on :
1   **Hue** - the actual pure colour eg red or blue
2   **Tint -** the level of white or black added
3   **Finish -** the surface effect eg matte or shiny
4   **Opacity -** the level of light permeation

Simple theories always appear more complex when written down, so the best way to understand how the theory works is to put it into practice and physically play with the paint.

hue

Pure hues (colours) contain no tint (white or black). The basic pure colour wheel is made up of **Primary colours** (red, yellow, blue) and **Secondary colours** (green, purple, orange). In the Colourise range, there are **cool (blue-toned), and warm (orange-toned)** versions of the primary shades, so that you can select a basic starter set in your preferred tone. **Colour saturation** describes the intensity of the colour, which is controlled by the amount of pigment.

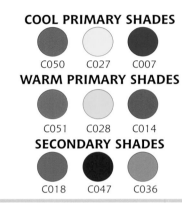

COOL PRIMARY SHADES
C050   C027   C007
WARM PRIMARY SHADES
C051   C028   C014
SECONDARY SHADES
C018   C047   C036

tint

Tints are shades that contain **varying levels of white or black.**
The addition of white or black makes the paint appear to be 'cloudier' ie; **more opaque,** and **less translucent**.
The **Semi-opaque** shades in the Colourise range are all tints.
Absolute Black and Absolute white are 100% tints, as they contain no other hue.

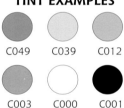

TINT EXAMPLES
C049   C039   C012
C003   C000   C001

finish

This is the **physical surface appearance** of the paint.

Available Stewart Gill paint finishes are :
matte (Colourise)
pearlescent (Pearlise & Alchemy)
metallic (Metamica & Byzantia)
glittery (Galactica).

matte   pearlescent

metallic   glittery

opacity

Opacity describes the **denseness of a colour in terms of light permeability.**

Transparent - 100% see-through.
The background is clearly visible, even if coloured, (ie; window glass allows full clarity).
Translucent - Semi-transparent.
The background is still visible, but clarity is reduced (ie; stained glass can still be seen through, but partially diffuses the view behind).
Semi-opaque - Denser coverage.
The background is barely visible, and clarity greatly reduced, (ie; frosted bathroom panels).
Opaque -100% block-out.
The background is totally obscured (ie; mirror glass).

Colour Mixing - How do I begin?

Following these simple colour-coded steps, you can easily create personalised shades that co-ordinate beautifully with your project. First, imagine the colour you want to create, then break it down into the four components of hue, tint, finish, and opacity. It's as easy as 1, 2, 3, 4...

"Hello - is that the Colour Doctor? - I desperately need HELP! I'd love to mix a slightly translucent shimmering pale turquoise-blue shade, to match my favourite shoes! - how can I make it myself?"

technique
BASIC COLOUR MIXING

Step 1 : hue

Decide what pure colour you will use as a starting point ie; what is the main descriptive part of the shade you want to create?
In the example given it is **turquoise-blue**.
Choose the colour from the COLOURISE range that is the closest match - it is usually best to start looking at the primary and secondary shades, as most shades can be mixed from these.

Step 2 : tint

Decide if you need white or black to lighten or darken.
To lighten the turquoise-blue, add a small amount of **White Colourise C001**. Remember that 'tints', are less translucent than 'hues', so in order to keep the shade as translucent as possible, just add a very small amount. Alternatively, you could omit the Colourise altogether, and choose a white shimmer product at Step 3, which would give a shimmer without being cloudy.

Step 3 : finish

Decide on the surface effect ie; iridescent shimmer
For a subtle shimmer add tiny amounts of **Pearlise White P01** or **Alchemy Seaspray A16W** into the mix. For shinier results add Metamica or Galactica instead.

Step 4 : opacity

Dilute with water or Extender Medium to decrease the opacity level.
We added a small amount of **water** for translucence.

Step 1: Mix Colourise Ultramarine with Lemon

(This makes dark turquoise)

Step 2 : Lighten with Pearlise White

(this makes pale shimmering turquoise)

Step 3 : Add Galactica Ocean for a turquoise sparkle

Step 4 : Dilute with water to make a translucent mix.

Layering the paints
KNOWING WHICH PRODUCTS TO USE, AND IN WHAT ORDER

Experimenting with direct layering techniques can create a wide spectrum of surface effects, as well as making more economical use of your products.

How opacity levels affect the layering order

It is vital to understand 'opacity' when using multimedia layering techniques, as products which are more opaque appear more dominant on the visual surface. The general principal is to apply your layers of colour according to the opacity levels, in a graduation from either opaque to translucent, or vice versa.

It is a good idea for the first few experiments to take all the products you intend to use, and sort them into an ascending order according to their opacity rating. This means you form a line of paints on the work table, starting with the most translucent ones, then the glazes, then the semi-opaques, and finally the opaques.

This line-up is the actual order you will use the products in, and you can choose whether you start with the translucent layers, or the opaque ones. Whichever end of the line you start with however, continue working in order along the line until you get to the other end. The chart below gives an indication of a layering order starting with the most translucent products through to the most opaque - this is my favourite way of working, but the reverse order is equally valid.

Stewart Gill paints are designed to intermix within the various ranges, but can also be layered directly onto the surface. The slight exception is Galactica, which is dulled if mixed with other paints, so for the sparkliest results, do not intermix but apply directly as a final layer.

Dominant and Recessive Layers

Which layering order you choose to work in depends on what you want to draw the most attention to. The top layers occupy a dominant position in any creative work, purely because they are physically nearer the visual surface, and closer to the eye. Dominant layers are like the Diva at the front of the stage that deservedly attracts the most attention. Be aware that sometimes your work may not look 'right' because a particular feature grabs the dominant position by default, and should really be on a recessive layer (ie; sent back to the chorus line!) Recessive layers are the background and middle layers which work together as a support for the top layers. They are a vitally important foundation, and must never be thought of as 'less important' than the dominant layers. When creating the recessive layers, always consider what will make a suitable contrast to the dominant layer that is still to come. Creating a distinct contrast between the recessive and dominant layers is a very effective way to ensure your surface really sings!

Examples

If the dominant position (top layer) has shiny, sparkly paints, then the background layers in contrast need to be matte, so attention is not drawn away from the surface. If the dominant position is a matte texture, then the background layers in contrast need to be either shiny, or smooth ie; multiple layers of thinly applied glazes, or even a highly polished matte backgound.

Layer	Suggested Products	Appearance	Method
BACKGROUND LAYERS	**Colourise**	Translucent matte	Fluid colour washes, solid blocks of colour or patterns
MIDDLE LAYERS	**Pearlise** **Alchemy**	Mid-Shiny, semi-opaque Interference Shine	Medium-concentration glazes over the background layers to create multi-directional depth where the background is still clearly visible
TOP LAYERS	**Metamica** **Byzantia** **Galactica**	High-Shine opaque High-Shine opaque Highly reflective	Detailed sharply-defined highlights that will pull the background and middle layers into focus
optional final layer	**Alchemy** **Colourise**	Interference Shine Translucent matte	Thin washes & glazes used sparingly to 'knock back' overly bright highlights, and areas that are too bold or attention-grabbing

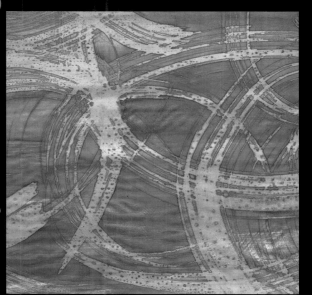

print pattern fashion textiles decoration plastics journals collage

Paint, Print & Pattern

It's time to make your mark! Using stamps, stencils, printing techniques, resists, or good old-fashioned hand painting, let your surfaces be adorned with pattern!

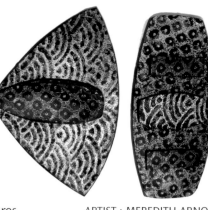

Be brave and experiment - try combining contrasting imagery, colours and textures in the same piece. You can always recycle the less-glorious attempts by cutting & collaging with stitch and more printing to create exciting new assemblages.

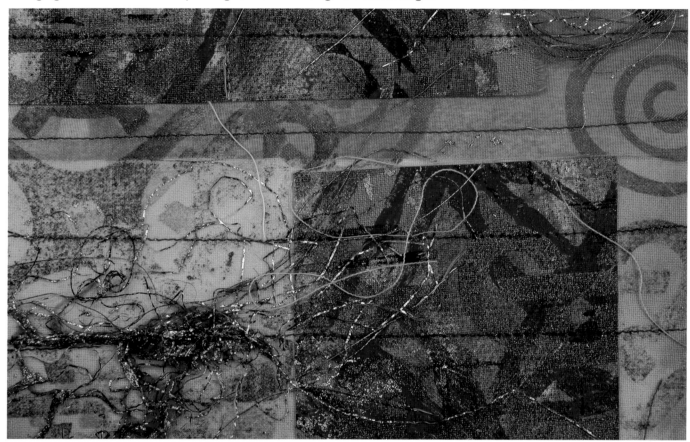

Above : *Sheer fabrics layered to expose under-printing, combined with top-level stitch & assemblage, add weighty surface interest to this delicate piece. Colourise C017, C032, C037, Alchemy A15A, A02E.*

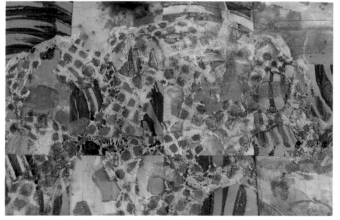

Below Left : *Geometric printed patterns on pieced blocks are liberated by the multimedia surface collage of layered print, stitch and paint techniques.* ***Below Right :*** *a highly effective yet simple study with Memostafo foam prints & outline stitching. Colourise C014, C027, C004, and Alchemy A07F, A16W.*

SAMPLES THIS PAGE CLOCKWISE DIRECTION

1. Watercolour & sponge techniques with *leaf-printing and hand embroidery. Colourise C037, C016.*

2. Partial-area stamping *using Artaglio PB13 on scraped background. C050, C028, C001, M002, BP05.*

3. Shrink Plastic Cushion Tags stencilled with Colourise *C032, C001, and Galactica G52, G7. Shrink tags embellished with embossing powder AE08, AE10.*

4. Paper Batik *resist technique with over-stamped painted squares. Colourise C051, Pearlise P01, Alchemy A10F, Galactica 3P, Metamica M001.*

5. Pelmet Vilene, water-coloured background, with stamping and embossing. Colourise C043, C036, C004, C001, Embossing AE08, Artaglio KS4

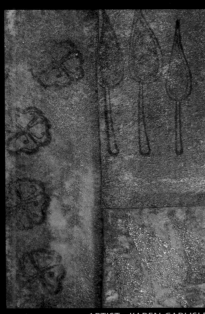

ARTIST : KAREN CARLISLE

ARTIST : JEAN BOATH

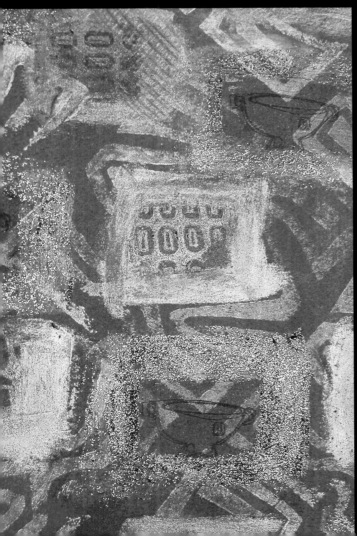

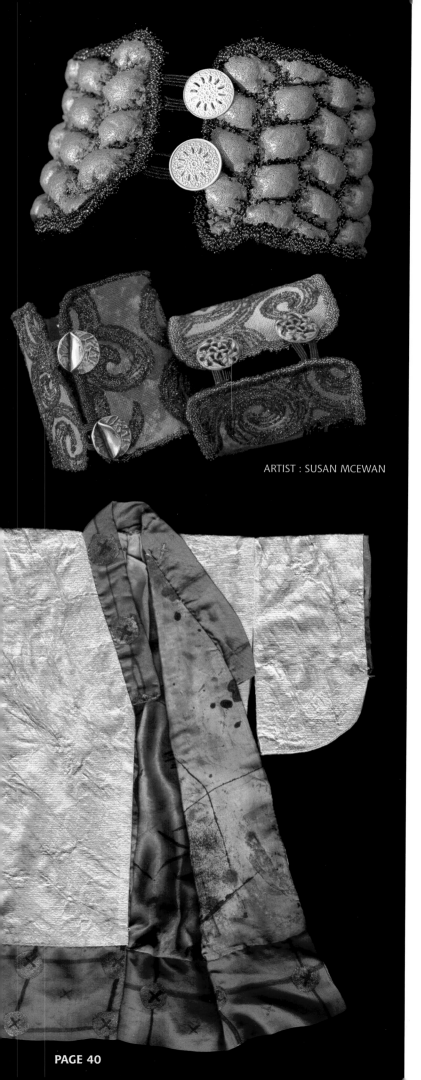

ARTIST : SUSAN MCEWAN

Fashion & Wearable Art

Now you can create stylish, individual pieces to add flair to your wardrobe.

Decorate your clothing, shoes, hats, or even make jewellery and bags. If you really want to put on a spectacular show of finery, you can use Stewart Gill to create evening & bridal couture, and dance & theatrical costumes.

Above : Funky Fashion T-shirt   ARTIST : LYNN WILD
Alchemy painted in rectangles, and stamped with rubber stamp fashion designs, beaded & embellished. Matching brooch made from shrink plastic.

Top Left : Cuffs - *painted & machine-embroidered canvas & rubber underlay. Colourise C044, C047, C030, C020, Metamica M001.*

Left : Silk Paper Kimono - *stencilled, painted & diffusion-sprayed silk lining with fusion paper. Colourise C008, C044, C037, Metamica M002.*

Right : Brooches using Intaglio Embossing technique. (Multiple layers of Ultragloss AE11 powder heated to produce a thick surface capable of impressing stamps into). Backgrounds created with stamps, Colourise, and Byzantia paints. Beads and wire added to embellish.

Below : Shrink Plastic Earrings stamped in Byzantia BP09, BP07. Edge highlights in Metamica M002.

ARTIST : ANNA JUSTICE

ARTIST : HELEN CHILTON

Above : Paperclay Brooch impressed with Artaglio PB13 stamps, air-dried, then dry-brushed with Colourise C014. Fresco Flakes FF09 glazed with Alchemy A11A, and embossing powders AE03, AE08, sprinkled & heated.

Below & Left : Painted Fabric Necklace stencilled with MSS03, stamped with Artaglio KS1, and painted with Byzantia BP02, Alchemy A08F, Colourise C000, C017.

ARTIST : SARAH LAWRENCE

Embellished Textiles

The painted surface can be a complete visual journey, or just the beginning layers of your exploration into additional decoration.

From basic colour washes through to detailed patterns, these first layers are an integral part of the design, not just a means of 'covering the white space'.
Your choices of imagery, colour, saturation and the actual physicality of the painted surface will direct the subsequent layers of embellishment.

On these next pages a variety of contemporary embroidery & quilting samples show varying levels of embellishment, from minimal outline stitching through to serious layers of three-dimensional textile assemblage. While most of the pieces are also functional items, they have been designed primarily from an aesthetic standpoint.

*Left : **Discharge Bleaching** with Colourise and free-motion embroidery.   **Middle : Glitterati Appliqué** fused fibre sheets appliquéd with painted fusible webbing, and machine embroidery.   **Right : Stencil & Stitch** Multiple layers of graduated stencils with free-motion quilting to highlight.*

ARTIST : FIONA KELLY

ARTIST : JENI OSBORNE

ARTIST : TONI HANLEY

Right and Below :
"Davy Jones' Locker"
Painted silk box with Glitterati
fibres fused underneath black
organza, machine-embroidered &
heavily beaded surface.

ARTIST : LIZ PATON

Below : Microscopic Textures
Painted background fabric of felted & fused threads &
Glitterati fibres, layered with sheer burnt fabrics and
Filigree Fluid line detail, and machine stitched rows.

ARTIST : LINDA COOPER

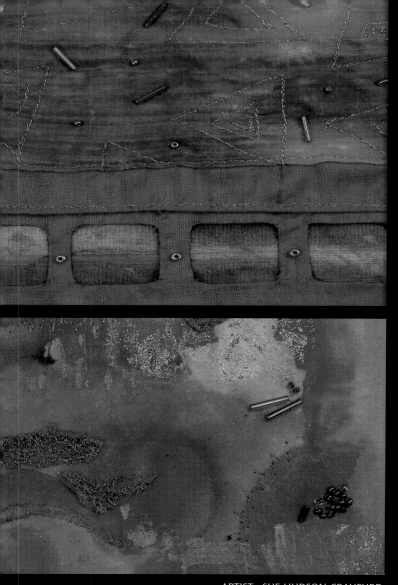

ARTIST : SUE HUDSON-CRAUFURD

Above : Silk painting with stitch (details)
Minimal use of surface embellishment does not detract from the vibrant colour which is successfully allowed to dominate these pieces.
Colourise C036, C043, C014, C050. Metamica M007, Galactica G52.

Above : Machine-embroidery with over-painting
A printed paper design was placed over silk fabric in an embroidery hoop and free-motion machine embroidered directly through the paper. After sewing, the paper was partially ripped away and remaining areas were over-painted with Byzantia BP01, BP03, and BP04.

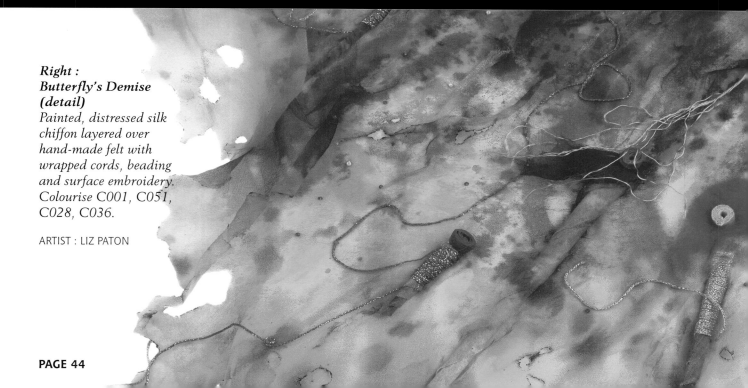

**Right :
Butterfly's Demise (detail)**
Painted, distressed silk chiffon layered over hand-made felt with wrapped cords, beading and surface embroidery.
Colourise C001, C051, C028, C036.

ARTIST : LIZ PATON

Above & Right : Embroidered Cushion (details)
Linen painted with colour wash and blend techniques using Colourise
C032, C028, C030, C044, C001. Heavy embroidery threads couched,
coiled and painted. Iridescent highlights painted in Alchemy A01E,
A06F, A18W, and Byzantia BP03, BP05.

Below : Screenprint with Stitched Highlights
Metamica M004 & M002 applied through a hand drawn screen-print for
sharp definition. Embroidered with stranded cotton hand-stitches for an
effective stylistic contrast.

Below : Beaded Byzantia Panel
Byzantia paints are the backdrop for
shining seed & bugle beads & metallic
machine embroidery - a good example of
building an intensely rich surface with
minimal products. BP03, BP04, BP06,
BP07, BP08, BP09.

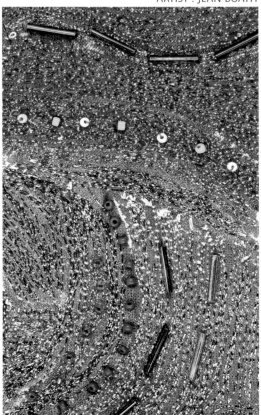

Surface Decoration

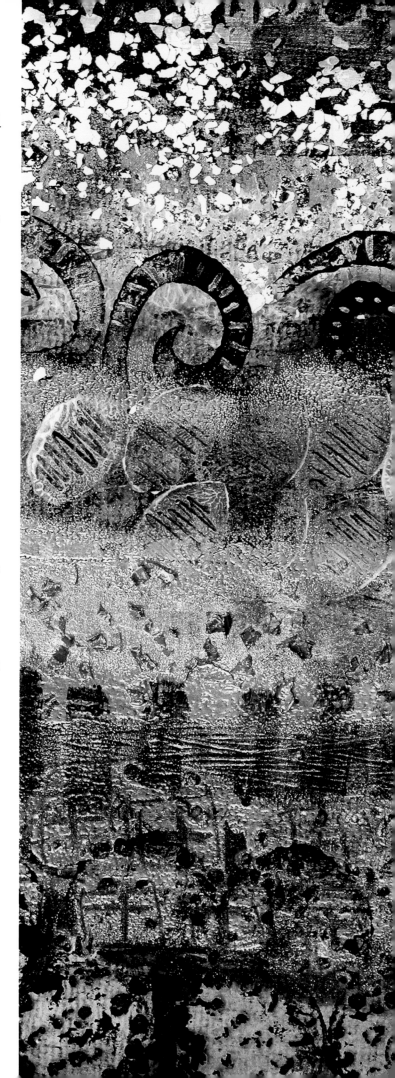

Adding interest to your surface is all a matter of how far you are prepared to go... Use any Effect product alone or in combination to create top-layer textures that truly deserve your visual attention.

Experiment with embedding flakes, chips, metal leaf, beads, threads & jewels into glues and paints.

Stack layers of translucent & transparent fabrics, papers and foils, to create glorious yet subtle depths of detail. Trap any of the Effects, or off-cuts of stitch, collage and memorabilia in between the layers for added interest and mystery.

Mix the paints with Filigree Fluid for coloured & raised texture, or simply over-paint once raised. Heated metallic paints make great textures in themselves (see page 12). Endless paint mixes are possible with mediums such as PVA, gesso, varnish, & latex . Experiment to create unique textures and glazes for dripping, casting, layering and highlights.

In addition, the embossing powders can be sprinkled over any worked surface for extra glimmer. The important thing is to have fun, and work that surface!

FACING PAGE (clockwise from top) :
Selection of Four Byzantia Swatches
Backgrounds painted with Byzantia Jeweltone paints. Filigree Fluid applied freehand and onto stamps, then covered with AE08 embossing powder. Artaglio stamps (PB14, KS5, RG1) randomly placed, impressed into thick Metamica for relief Bubble & Blister technique.

Right - Plastic Lamination
Clear & coloured transparent plastics layered with foils, sheer fabrics, threads and Glitterati fibres, then machine stitched randomly to secure and decorate.

Left - Winter Collage
Colourise background sponged (C014, C000, C001), and Fresco Flakes (FF08) sprinkled into paint while wet. 'Flowers of Scotland - Winter' stamp painted with Byzantia (BP06,07,08) & Pearlise (P02).

THIS PAGE : textures created from foam stamps, scratching, thick paint, flakes & embossing powder.

ARTIST : LINDA COOPER

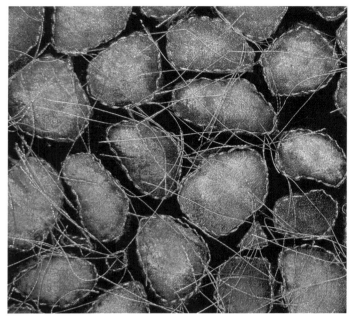

ARTIST : FIONA KELLY

ARTIST : FIONA KELLY

Clockwise from top :
Alchemy White *paints stencilled through Giraffe MSA05, then machine quilted with metallic threads which are deliberately left untrimmed for detail.*

Squares & Lines - *Layers of Metamica scratched to reveal underneath paint colours.*

Distressed Beach Huts - *Artaglio KS1 stamped over a tissue and Fresco Flakes background, with Colourise washes.*

Filigree SeaFoam - *Filigree Fluid mixed with Glitterati, pressure-ironed through teflon, then machine-appliquéd.*

Clockwise from top :
Metamica and Colourise *on a variety of plastic &
rubber surfaces, zig-zag stitched, and heated to distress.*

Filigree Fluid Colourwash - *Colourise washed to blend a
background. Filigree Fluid applied with foam stamps and
heated to raise, then over-buffed with Metamica M02
Brass. (Same technique used in bottom right swatch).*

Archaelogical surfaces - *Wool felt and heavy interlining
painted with Colourise, Metamica and Galactica. The
surface was 'aged' with machine-embroidery and soldering
iron burns, to create holes and ragged edges.*

Skeletal Expansion - *Filigree Fluid applied onto a
painted textile background, with a spatula through a MS
stencil (Zebra MSA01). Heated to expand, then painted
with Metamica & Galactica when cool.*

Shining Textures - *Gilding Chips & metal leafing
embedded into roughly swirled Byzantia paints.*

ARTIST : JENI OSBORNE

ARTIST : SUSAN MCEWAN

ARTIST : FIONA SHORTMAN

ARTIST : TRUDI TROUPE

ARTIST : KAREN CARLISLE

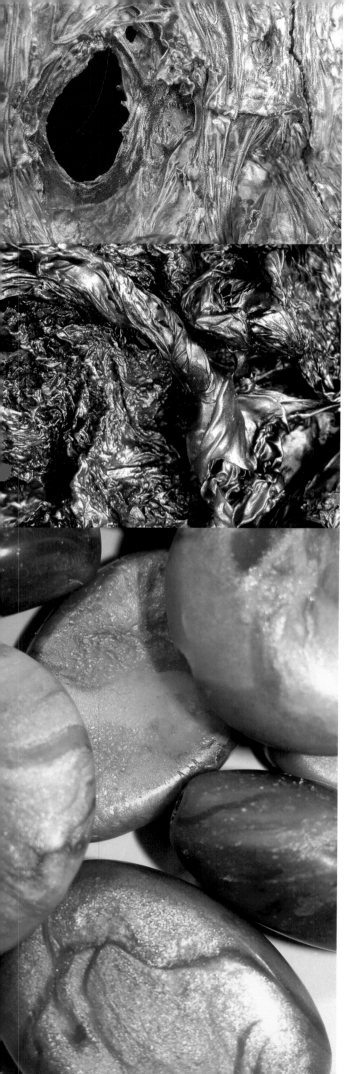

Plastics & Polymers

Many plastic materials utilise heat to achieve hardening, distortion, or shrinking.

Stewart Gill paints are formulated to be permanent on porous surfaces, but they are also heat-responsive, which allows increased permanence on some non-porous surfaces.
You do not need to make any changes to the heating process of these materials - the paint will not affect the way that the polymer / plastic reacts to heat.

Lightly sand flat plastic sheets and shrink plastic with ultra-fine emery-grade paper, to make the surface more receptive to the paint. Be careful when heating as plastics can give off fumes, and are susceptible to burning.

Experiment with many different plastic materials, such as ; polymer clays, Tyvec ®, plastic bags, bubble wrap, Glitterati, cellophane, closed-cell foams, polystyrene, vinyl underlay and sheet products, shrink plastic, hot-laminating plastic, and nylon and polyester fabrics.

Polymer clay & Shrink plastic can be painted either before or after baking. When baking or heating, use the standard times & temperatures as recommended by the individual product manufacturers. If the pieces are painted prior to baking, the results are permanent and can even be safely washed without losing surface colour. If you paint your plastics after heating, protect the surface by using a heat-gun to 'quick-fix' the paint; or seal with a coat of varnish after drying; or sprinkle embossing powders onto the wet paint and heat to seal.

Top Left : Painted & Stitched Plastics   ARTIST : PENNY USHER
These gloriously vibrant sculptures are in fact recycled carrier bags assembled with stitch, heavily painted, then heated to distort.

All polymer beads on this page :
Conditioned and flattened clay blended with Byzantia paints, moulded into beads and holes pierced, then baked to harden. After cooling, the clay was sanded with ultrafine sand-paper to give a gleaming polished surface.

ARTISTS : inside back cover

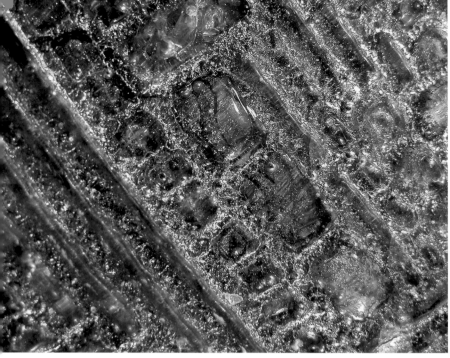

ARTIST : LIZ PATON

Above & Left : Spacestation Brooch
A mount-board shape was painted with Metamica, and embossed with multiple layers of Ultragloss clear embossing powder AE11. Micro beads were added to the final layer, and impressed with Artaglio stamp PB12 to raise a relief.

Below : Cathedral Brooch
Shrink plastic shape decorated with Colourise, shrunk and flattened. Block-embossing and colour-dusting with interference shades and PolyGlitter to finish.

ARTIST : KAREN CARLISLE

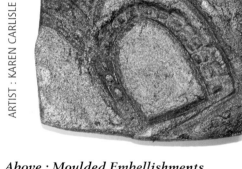

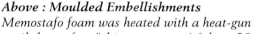

Above : Moulded Embellishments
Memostafo foam was heated with a heat-gun until the surface "shines or sweats' (about 20 seconds). Artaglio KS4 was then stamped into the warm foam, which moulds to the shape of the stamp. When cool, the pieces were painted with Metamica (MM02, MM07, & MM08). This technique is ideal for cards, scrapbooks, jewellery, costumery, or as stitchable embellishments for textile wall-art.

Below : Shrink Plastic Neckace with eraser stamp
A hand-carved eraser was used to both print the image and create the relief texture by pressing hard into the plastic while still hot after shrinking.
Note that a thin layer of paint will give a more intense colour on shrink plastic, and thickly applied paint creates a ruffled texture.

ARTIST : SARAH LAWRENCE

Papercrafts

From subtle to vivid colours, thin to thick textures, and realistic to abstract patterns, there are endless ways to produce gorgeous surfaces for paper & card projects.

Above : Cityscape ARTIST : TERRY CRELLIN
Pearlise diluted with water and drawn through calligraphic ink pens onto a Colourise wash base.
Right (top to bottom):
Dilute Colourise with Galactica for pretty painted frames around embossed stamped images.
Paisley & Flower Box ARTIST : GLENDA WATERWORTH
Rubberstamping on acetate, vellum & card, using the painted acetate as a transfer resist. Box lid painted with Byzantia, then covered with Gilding Chips. A metallic sticker pressed on top and sealed under a thick layer of AE11clear embossing powder.
Victorian Lady Card ARTIST : SHONA ADAMS
Rubber stamped image tinted with C047 Colourise, & Alchemy A12A paint. Miniature vellum envelope 'sealed' with AE02 interference embossing powder.
Paper Batik Weaving *technique shown on page 10, cut and woven, ready for stitching, laminating etc...*

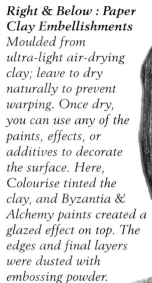

Right & Below : Paper Clay Embellishments
Moulded from ultra-light air-drying clay; leave to dry naturally to prevent warping. Once dry, you can use any of the paints, effects, or additives to decorate the surface. Here, Colourise tinted the clay, and Byzantia & Alchemy paints created a glazed effect on top. The edges and final layers were dusted with embossing powder.

Above : Silent Muse   ARTISTS : students from CCI, UK.
Paper maché sculpture, dried naturally, then painted with Colourise, and highlights applied with Metamica and Patina Embossing Powder BE02, BE03.

Colour-dusting with embossing powder is an effective way to create simulated ceramics, without the weight - so use paper clay embellishments for cards, altered books, and costumes where you need deceptively lightweight pieces.

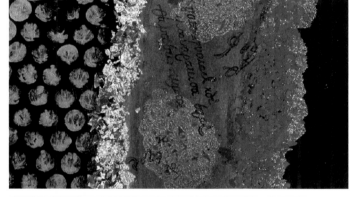

Left & Below : Paper Surface Designs
By understanding the different technical qualities of art products, you can create a myriad of amazing surfaces from a minimal number of techniques. Try combining ideas from both the sections in this book, to design your own unique papers for scrapbooks, cards, gifts, or interior projects.

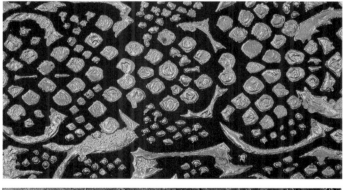

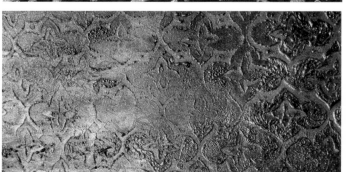

ARTIST : GLENDA WATERWORTH

Books, Journals & Collage

Shrink Plastic Book : *bound with craft wire. Uses Colourise & Alchemy paints and Black Label Embossing powders.*

Be true to traditional book arts, or venture into multimedia collage techniques...whatever your leaning, you can achieve stunning book works with paint and collage.

Whether you create books for recording & retrieving information, or as personal journals & visual diaries, or as contemporary fine art; allow the materials to find their own voice. Playing extensively with your art materials will create a reservoir of ideas and techniques that will enrich and enliven the surfaces.

If your book focuses mainly on exploring the mediums and surfaces, then different experiments and eclectic styles can be successfully collaged together into one piece, without worrying too much about the deep & meaningful stuff. However, if your book is to present a congruent, clear, visual message, then choose the techniques & materials carefully to actively promote the intention behind your artwork (ie; a beach themed book could include a driftwood cover, paint mixed with sand, and real dried-seaweed prints).

Consider the book medium as much more than just the sum of it's materials - it is the perfect arena for your personal ethos to be borne out into a physical entity, custom-designed so every material aspect truly supports the meaning. Opening and reading a special hand-made book is a journey into a sacred inner world, for explorations into your personal history, philosophy, emotions, memory and imagination are celebrated with each turn of the painted page...

Multimedia workbooks ARTIST : LINDA COOPER   *Handmade printed papers - RG*

...there is a certain essence of integrity in the rough unaltered state of our workbooks that can be incredibly beautiful, yet prone to disappearing before we can trap it in the final art piece...

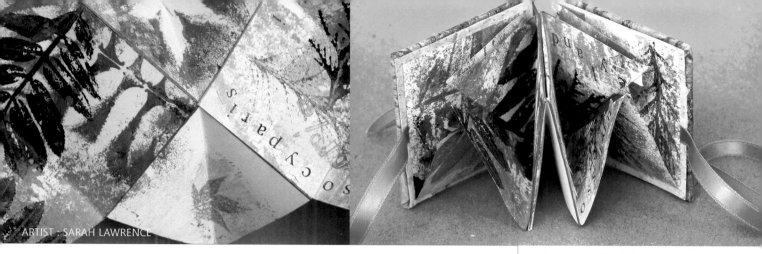

*Above : **Multi-fold Leaf Print Book*** *using Alchemy, Colourise, and letter transfers on card and fabric.*

*Left : **Postcards from Byzantia Assemblage** - using Artaglio KS stamps, Colourise, Metamica and pencil, to create small cityscape mementos on watercolour paper, and assembled into a 3-way album with the postcards loosely 'bound' as pages.*

*Below Right : **Landflag** CD book using RG3 & RG4 Artaglio stamps, Colourise, Fresco Flakes and pastels. The CD box houses mount-board 'covers' which become the pages, and the transparent insert 'pages' become the spine. Stitched fabric front cover uses Byzantia & Colourise .*

Above :
Byzantia Collage Book
an assortment of painted background papers collaged with diecuts, and painted polymer clay emblem on cover.
Uses Byzantia paints, Filigree Fluid.

last words

My favourite things : Art-kit list

Everyone has their own little obsessions - for us artsy-crafty folk it's the huge kit bag of essential stuff that we lug about everywhere through life!

This page lists the creative stuff I simply can't do without, the pared-down range of products I always take with me when teaching or travelling. It's important to remind any friends/family/partners that don't understand our obsession, that this list is diminutive compared to a true shopaholics' fantasy spree involving shoes & handbags! (However, if you're anything like me, you're probably dangerously drawn to those too!)

stewart gill paints & stuff

COLOURISE C050, C007, C028, C043, C047, C017, C030, C044, C021

ALCHEMY A01E, A06F, A11A, A16W

METAMICA M002, M003, M007

PEARLISE P01, P10

GALACTICA GRB & G322

BLACK LABEL AE08, AE09, AE10, AE11

BYZANTIA + choose one interference white shade

Honestly, they're so fabulous I have them all, but recommend choosing 1-2 shades first.

EFFECTS Choose one matching shade each, plus Fresco Flakes FF08 & FF10

ADDITIVES Filigree fluid & Beadhesive

TOOLS TW09, LF05, LF06

GLITTERATI choose 1 fibre shade, & 1 contrasting film.

other fun(damental) stuff

BRUSHES **Windsor & Newton** 'Galleria', **Loew Cornell** 'Golden Taklon', **Scharff** 'White Nylon' & 'Aqua Flow', **Royal** 'Soft-Grip', **Daler Rowney** 'Cryla'.

ROUND #'s 0, 2 & 8. FILBERTS - 1/4 " & 3/4" SQUARE TIP #'s 4/6 & 10/12 +one large brush approx 3-4" wide, from a DIY store.

INKPADS **Crafters** Black Mini, **Top Boss** Clear Mini. **Cut 'n' Dry** foam sheets, and **Clearsnap** Colorbox blank pads, for making paint pads

DRAWING **Fabrico** Black dual-tip pen. 6B drawing pencils, **Aquarelles**. **Caran d'Ache** Neocolour II water soluble pastels.

TAPE Masking - 12, 25, 50mm. Double-sided.

TOOLS Separate scissors for fabric & paper. Travel-iron. **Clearsnap** Colorbox Stylus Tool & tips. Single hole paper punch. Awl for book-binding. **Polyshrink** Sanding block. Sponges & Rags.

GLUES **Helmar 450** Universal craft glue. Glue dots. Foam mounts. **3M** SprayMount

PAPER & FABRIC **Daler Rowney** acid free landscape format journals. Watercolour papers, vellum, Tyvec, 100% cotton sheeting, 100% cotton velvet, 100% silk crepe. Roclon Craft Cotton. Pelmet vilene, Iron-on Inter-lining. Appliqué fusing.

highly recommended

Here's some more items that I find indispensible, or just totally love the quality and need to rave about!

Disclaimer : the recommendations and products listed here are my personal feelings entirely and are unsolicited, unendorsed and unwarranted by the manufacturers stated, or Stewart Gill Ltd. All brand names stated are acknowledged as the ©, ™ or ® property of the stated manufacturers and their respective companies.

Roclon (USA) fabrics - these are perfect for crafting as they don't fray, don't roll or wrinkle, and have a luminous white surface that really brings out the best in paint colours. You can stitch, punch, glue, paint, everything!

Lakeland Ltd (UK) Magic Oven Liner This sheet is amazingly thick and large, to protect your surface from all heat sources. The best quality & value I've tried ever.

Vilene - a wide range of inter-linings and stiffeners which are great bases for books, card crafts, jewellery & costumery.

Kato Polyclay (USA)- a remarkable polymer clay, as it holds it's elastic shape without distorting, making it easy to apply paint on. Plus the colour range is pure, and accepts paint beautifully, rendering the colours accurately without clouding.

Eberhard Faber (Germany) EfaPlast 'Soft & Light' air-dry clay - this version is very light, not sticky, and has minimal shrinking or warping upon drying.

Lucky Squirrel Polyshrink (USA) - the original and still the best as far as I'm concerned - pieces maintain the original ratio after shrinking, without distortion.

*And a special thanks goes to **Bernina Sewing Machines (Switzerland)**, for all the metal chassis models, particularly my beloved 1230... it's gonna last forever.*

'Harvest' from the Flowers of Scotland Rubberstamp Series, by Mary Stewart.